NEW DIRECTIONS
FOR METHODOLOGY OF
SOCIAL AND
BEHAVIORAL SCIENCE

Number 8 • 1981

# NEW DIRECTIONS FOR METHODOLOGY OF SOCIAL AND BEHAVIORAL SCIENCE

A Quarterly Sourcebook
Donald W. Fiske, Editor-in-Chief

Number 8, 1981

# Generalizing from Laboratory to Life

Irwin Silverman
Editor

Jossey-Bass Inc., Publishers
San Francisco • Washington • London

GENERALIZING FROM LABORATORY TO LIFE
*New Directions for Methodology of Social and Behavioral Science*
Number 8, 1981
    Irwin Silverman, Editor

*New Directions for Methodology of Social and Behavioral Science*
is published quarterly by Jossey-Bass Inc., Publishers.
Subscriptions are available at the regular rate for institutions,
libraries, and agencies of $30 for one year. Individuals may
subscribe at the special professional rate of $18 for one year.

*Correspondence:*
Subscriptions, single-issue orders, change of address notices,
undelivered copies, and other correspondence should be sent to
*New Directions* Subscriptions, Jossey-Bass Inc., Publishers,
433 California Street, San Francisco, California 94104.

Editorial correspondence should be sent to the Editor-in-Chief,
Donald W. Fiske, University of Chicago, Chicago, Illinois 60637.

Library of Congress Catalogue Card Number LC 80-84295
International Standard Serial Number ISSN 0271-1249
International Standard Book Number ISBN 87589-852-1

Cover design by Willi Baum
Manufactured in the United States of America

# Contents

# Editor's Notes

Many might agree that generalizability from laboratory to life is the most formidable methodological issue for behavioral science; certainly it has been the most extensively and intensively discussed. Behavioral science is not unique in this regard. The issue is an inevitable complication of the search for firmer laws of causality—and the attendant transition from descriptive to experimental methods—in most disciplines. Behavioral science may be unique, however, in the philosophical attention given to the matter. Beyond the pure methodological problems of how to increase generalizability, we have been drawn into such meta-issues as where the separation begins between behavior *in vitro* and *in vivo* and whether it is fruitful to confront the issue at all. It is not surprising, then, that four of these six authors—Bakan, Bugelski, Jung, and Silverman— have elected to approach the question mainly in this broader vein and that each has done so from quite different perspectives. Complementing these contributions, the chapters by Lefcourt and others and McClintock focus on more concrete considerations of generalizability in the areas of clinical and comparative psychology, respectively. Perhaps more questions are raised than are answered, but that is probably an accurate reflection of the state of the field.

Irwin Silverman
Editor

*Irwin Silverman is professor of psychology,*
*York University, Ontario.*

*Studies show that rodents in simplified environments exhibit*
*copulatory behavior that differs from the behavior*
*of rodents in more naturalistic settings.*

# Simplicity from Complexity: A Naturalistic Approach to Behavior and Neuroendocrine Function

## Martha K. McClintock

Many aspects of the relationship between behavior and neuroendocrine function are unclear, and many apparent paradoxes remain unexplained. Part of the confusion stems from the use of laboratory environments that, although small and convenient, bear little resemblance to the natural environments of the animal studied.

The copulatory behavior of rodents is remarkably stereotyped when they mate in a standard laboratory testing cage. Because the behavior is so stable and replicable in this simple environment, it is tempting to use this model for investigating the neuroendocrine mechanisms of mating behavior. In fact, our understanding of the relationship between reproductive behavior and neuroendocrinology is based on the study of rodents in this simple environment. However, in an effort to control variation, researchers have arbitrarily

The work presented in this chapter was supported in part by grant no. BNS 78-03658 from the National Science Foundation.

restricted both to the point that they barely resemble the context in which rodents evolved. Therefore, it may be misguided to assume that the stereotypy and organization of behavior observed in the standard laboratory testing cage are properties of the organism. Some features of this behavior may be due to the unusual environment and therefore unlikely to have a simple or lawful relationship with neuroendocrine mechanisms.

Furthermore, some features of behavior are epiphenomena and not the direct product of a neuroendocrine mechanism. Nonetheless, they may be very salient in some environments. Thus although strong correlations have been established between the salient features of copulation in a standard laboratory environment and hormone levels or drug administration, it is not yet clear whether these particular features are directly related to neuroendocrine function. If mating could be observed in a variety of environments, it would be possible to identify the features that are robust or stable and thus more likely to be part of the mechanisms which directly coordinate behavior and neuroendocrine systems.

With these reservations in mind, we and others have undertaken the study of reproductive behavior in a variety of different environments. Realizing that behavior and neuroendocrine systems were naturally selected to be coordinated under a specific set of environmental conditions, we chose to include some features of these natural environments in the laboratory. Although this decision made observation conditions more complex and prevented direct control over the animals' interactions, we were able to rely on the animal's behavior, as it structured its environment itself, to elucidate the simple and lawful relationships that underlie the coordination of mating behavior and neuroendocrine function.

## Mating Among Rodents: Basic Questions and Paradoxes

When an investigator wishes to study the neuroendocrine mechanisms of rodent mating, a male and female are taken from different parts of the laboratory colony and put together in a small aquarium-like enclosure, which is often no larger than two feet square and devoid of anything but sawdust. In this barren environment, a pair of rats copulates in a pattern that is extremely stable. After some mutual sniffing and nuzzling, the male chases the female and mounts her rump by grasping her flanks and palpating them with his forepaws. If the female is in heat and receptive to mating, she responds to this stimulation with a strong dorsiflexion of her spine and a deflection of her tail; she adopts the posture called lordosis, which enables the male to achieve an intromission. After rapid thrusting, the male dismounts and usually grooms his penis immediately. The female rat may hold her lordotic posture for a moment after the dismount, and then she runs away. The pair repeats this interaction several times, having several intromissions in a row at one-minute intervals. Sometimes the male mounts the female without having intromission; nonetheless, he almost always achieves several intromissions before finally ejaculating. After the male ejaculates, he becomes quiescent, sits or lies on the floor of the cage, and emits a 22 kHz ultrasonic call. After a three- or four-minute rest, the rats resume mating. The male may have as many as seven of these ejaculatory series in a single copulatory session.

Other rodents exhibit minor variations on this basic copulatory pattern of multiple intromissions and ejaculations (Dewsbury, 1975b). For example, the female hamster has a lordosis reflex that is unusual in its strength and rigidity. Odors and ultrasounds from the male hamster, as well as palpation of her flanks, can elicit a lordotic posture in the female that is so rigid she can be picked up and set down in another cage without losing lordosis or altering her posture (Beach and others, 1976; Floody and Pfaff, 1977).

The questions are: What neuroendocrine mechanisms control these copulatory behaviors and what functions do they serve? For instance, from the male's perspective, what determines the number of intromissions that he will have before reaching ejaculation? Why does he have multiple intromissions before ejaculating, and why so many ejaculations? An interrelationship between these two features of the male's copulatory pattern has already been established; the interval between his intromissions determines the total number he will have before reaching ejaculation. For example, if the interval between intromissions is artificially lengthened to three minutes (this is accomplished by removing the female and then returning her after a specified interval), a male in a standard laboratory cage will have only one half the usual preejaculatory intromissions of a male mating without interference at one-minute intervals. If the interval is lengthened to six or seven minutes, the number of preejaculatory intromissions increases again (Larsson, 1956). Thus, two to three minutes is the optimal interval for bringing a male to ejaculation. This finding raises other questions: Why do males consistently mate at intervals that are significantly shorter than the optimum set by their neuroendocrine systems? Why isn't there a better match between the temporal parameters of their behavior and the temporal parameters of the neuroendocrine reflex? What function is served by this lawful relationship between the timing of a male's copulatory behavior and its amount?

Further, in the small testing cage, the male's approaches appear to pace copulation. His behavior is encephalized; it is more than a simple reflex and must be fine-tuned to compensate for variability in the female's response. The female's behavioral repertoire, however, is restricted to the lordosis reflex and a dart-hop gait, which are integrated on a spinal and subcortical level. Thus, there appears to be a striking sex difference in the encephalization of sexual behavior, a sex difference that is echoed by apparent sex differences in the pharmacology of sexual motivation: The male's mounting behavior is reduced by interference with dopaminergic function while the female's lordosis reflex is enhanced (Caggiula and others, 1979). What accounts for such a striking sex difference in the neuroendocrine basis of sexual motivation?

Last, what evidence is there that this stereotyped sequence of behavior has anything to do with an organization of behavior that solved the problems of successful reproduction in a natural habitat? Beach, one of the first investigators of rodent copulation, focuses on this problem in an amusing but pointed essay entitled "The Snark Was a Boojum" (1950), and Kavenau (1964, p. 490) asserts that "domestic animals remain convenient vegetalized strains for physiological studies, but only wild animals provide the full range and rigor of response upon which solutions to the central problems of behavior must be based." Despite these early admonitions, current research continues to focus on domestic animals and perhaps makes impossible a clear understanding of the coordination of behavior and neuroendocrine function.

## Complicating the Physical Environment

Recognizing that neither copulatory behavior nor its neuroendocrine mechanisms evolved to mediate reproduction in a small cage, we have studied rodent copulation in a variety of environments that contain features of the natural environment and features of the environment in which laboratory strains were domesticated. Calhoun (1962) describes the burrow system and runways of wild rats in great detail. We used these specifications to construct in the laboratory a seminatural environment that had a burrow of runways, an open area with rocks and sticks, and leaves and woodchips for modifying the burrow (see Figure 1). As food and water were available at will, the rats did not have to expend much energy obtaining food, although they did spend time hoarding it. This important feature is probably atypical of many environments, but not unlike the abundant food supplies that are temporarily available in corn ricks and grain silos where wild rats prosper (Davis, 1951).

Our subjects were not placed into this environment just at the time of mating; instead, they were allowed to adapt to each other and to the physical environment for at least three days. Also, the females all came into a natural heat as the result of a spontaneous estrous cycle rather than a heat induced by sequential hormone injections. Therefore we lost direct control over the time when the female came into heat and mating began.

Some features of copulation remained the same in this seminatural environment; some, however, were entirely different. The females all displayed a behavior not recognized previously in the small cage. There, the male appeared to initiate copulation by chasing the female. Here, during mating in the larger open area, the males rarely approached the female. Instead the

## Figure 1. A Seminatural Laboratory Environment
### for Norway Rats

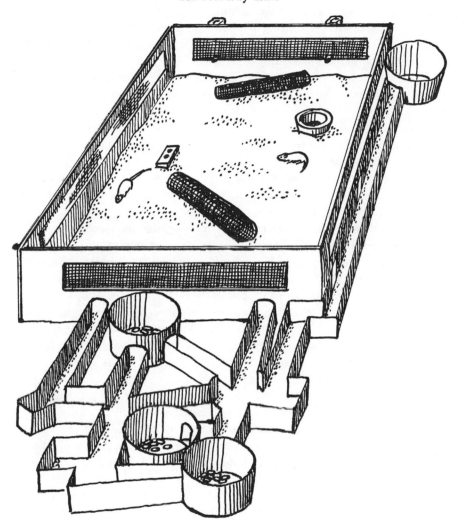

female initiated most mounts and intromissions by soliciting the male (McClintock and Adler, 1978). This female solicitation was new to the observers, was readily recognizable, and occurred in a variety of forms representing minor variations on a basic pattern (Hedricks and McClintock, forthcoming). Unless they were actively negotiating copulation, the male and female usually remained separated by at least three or four body lengths, a distance that is unobtainable in a small cage. The female would begin a solicitation by approaching the male. Once she was within one or two body lengths, she would nose or sniff the male, grooming his head or anogenital area. The male would also groom the female. The female would then abruptly orient herself away from the male and run away, sometimes with a darting and hopping gait. The male would then follow the female, chasing her until he mounted her. This pattern of female solicitation preceded 90 percent of the intromissions. Thus, intromissions rarely occurred unless they were solicited by a female.

In the small cage, the female is constantly kept within one or two body lengths of the male. She is therefore essentially trapped within the orientation component of her solicitation, and from the male's perspective, it probably appears that the female is constantly soliciting him. Therefore, because the small cage prevents the female from regulating the pacing of mating as she normally would, the male has the largest role in determining whether or not copulation occurs. However, we found that when the female is released from this confinement her solicitation behavior gives her a major role in determining the pacing of copulation.

Female solicitation appears to have neuroendocrine mechanisms different from the traditional measures of female sexual motivation: the lordosis reflex and the dart-hop gait. For example, females mating at a postpartum estrus have a different hormonal balance than females mating at a cycling estrus. This is correlated with a change in the pacing of solicitations and active sexual behaviors, even though there is no alternation in the reflexive measures of sexual motivation (Hedricks and McClintock, forthcoming). The discovery of female solicitation also suggests that there may not be a sex difference in the degree of cortical involvement during mating. In other words, it is the female's solicitation, not her lordosis reflex or dart-hop gait, that is functionally comparable to the male's approaches and mounts. Therefore, if the neuroendocrine mechanisms of solicitation are investigated, it may be found that they are similar to mechanisms in the male, and that the apparent sex differences in the neuroendocrine basis of sexual motivation are the spurious result of an inappropriate comparison, generated by a limited view of the female's behavioral repertoire.

We were able to verify our impression of female control of the pacing of mating by studying wild Norway rats (McClintock and Adler, 1978). This strategy not only allowed us to compare the copulatory pattern of the domestic strain with the wild strain but also allowed us to use this comparison to assess the relative contributions of the male and the female to the pace of mating.

We found that wild rats had a sequence of solicitation and copulation that was qualitatively similar to the domestic strain's. Thus, in a seminatural environment, the white laboratory rat still has a behavioral repertoire comparable to that of wild rats. In a similar finding, Price (1980) reports that the mating and aggressive behavior of domestic males is comparable to that of the wild males, if the environment gives them the opportunity. Therefore, the behavior of the domestic strain is not as impoverished as Kavenau (1964) would have us believe. However, while qualitatively similar, the copulatory behavior of the two strains was not identical. Wild pairs paced their intromissions at much longer intervals and had three times as many intromissions before ejaculation.

Next we observed the mating pattern of mixed-strain pairs and were surprised to find that a domestic male paired with a wild female had just as many intromissions before ejaculation as a wild male did. However, when a wild male was paired with a domestic female, he mated in the domestic pattern and had only one third the number of preejaculatory intromissions. Therefore, although it had been assumed that the number of preejaculatory intromissions was a male trait, we have demonstrated that it is in fact determined by the strain of the female with which the male mates. On the level of individual behavior, the female accomplished this control by pacing her solicitations for intromissions. Wild females paced intromissions more slowly than the domestic females and therefore received many more intromissions before the male ejaculated.

Female control over the number of the male's preejaculatory intromissions may seem paradoxical at first. However, multiple intromissions from the male are essential for successful pregnancy. If sperm is simply placed at the cervix of a female rat, conception will not occur. The female needs intromissions to stimulate the neuroendocrine mechanisms of sperm transport and to induce the progestational state which is necessary to support implantation. The number of intromissions and their temporal pattern are critical; if there are too few intromissions or if they occur too quickly, fertilization and implantation will not occur.

Thus, in the small testing cage, the environment takes over for the female, keeping the pair in proximity and producing a pace of intromissions that is sufficient for successful reproduction. However, the female has not always been able to rely on her environment to keep the male close and to pace copulation in concert with her neuroendocrine requirements. Therefore, in larger and more complex environments, the female actively regulates the distance between herself and the male, the temporal pattern and amount of mating that she requires for successful pregnancy. Strain differences in the rate of solicitation presumably reflect strain differences in the temporal parameters of their neuroendocrine systems.

Originally, we assumed that the female solicitation just required more space. However, when we simply increased the size of our testing environments, the male still approached the female repeatedly and the pacing of mating was fast, similar to that in the small cage. The female was occupied with avoiding the male, rather than regulating when she approached him. With the addition of a few barriers and rocks that created structural complexity in the environment, the female's solicitation behavior reemerged and the rate of copulation slowed to that which we had seen in our original seminatural environment. This suggests, then, that the environment must be physically and perhaps visually complex for a balanced interaction of mating to occur.

Ciaccio and others (1979) modified the standard testing environment of golden hamsters (*Mesocricetus auratus*) in a research strategy that is similar to ours. Recognizing that hamsters live underground, he created an environment that would allow them to dig a burrow but still permit observation while they were underground. He did this by providing a thin slice of earth bounded by clear plexiglass, an environment similar to the ant farms that many children have. He found that the female hamster dug a burrow and lived in it by herself. When the female was not in heat she defended this burrow vigorously against the male. However, as she came into heat, she marked the area around the burrow entrance with vaginal and glandular secretions, attracted the male, and led him down into the chamber of her burrow. She would then go back up to seal the entrance and return to the male. Once in the chamber, the female braced herself against the lip of her burrow and, as the male mounted her, she would take her characteristically rigid lordosis posture. Her immobility made mating easier under the confined conditions of the underground chamber, and the problems of predators and mate choice were solved by sealing the burrow entrance and blocking the male's exit route.

Thus, the lordosis reflex has differentiated to conform to the particular environments in which these two species mate: in the extreme confinement of a burrow chamber, in the case of the golden hamster; and in the open areas of dumps, ghetto lots, and river banks, in the case of the Norway rat.

## Complicating the Social Environment

While complicating the physical environment drew some aspects of copulatory behavior into line with neuroendocrine function, it did not resolve all paradoxes. For example, the pacing of intromissions has different consequences for the two sexes. From the male's perspective, the pace of intromissions affects the number of intromissions that he will have before reaching ejaculation; from the female's perspective, the pace affects the sperm transport necessary for conception and the release of progesterone necessary to support pregnancy. This functional difference is not particularly puzzling in and of itself, as it represents an efficient coordination between a male and female sharing the common goal of reproduction. However, the optimal pace for achieving these ends is different for the two sexes: domestic males reach ejaculation most quickly if intromissions are paced at two to three minutes (Larsson, 1956), while the optimal interval for inducing a progestational state in the female is closer to ten minutes, substantially longer than the interval that is most efficient for bringing a male to ejaculation (Edmonds and others, 1972). Furthermore, in a standard laboratory testing cage, pairs mate at one-minute intervals, faster than the optimum for either sex.

This apparent paradox was intensified by our observations that domestic males and females have had opposite responses to the identical selection pressure, namely domestication and selection for high reproductive yield. In the mixed-strain matings described before, we found that domestication has decreased the intervals at which females prefer to mate, while it has increased the intervals at which the domestic males prefer to mate. Given this sex difference in the response to domestication, the optimal interval for inducing a progestational state in wild females is probably even greater than it is in domestic females, and the optimal interval for promoting ejaculation in the wild males is probably even smaller. Thus, it appears that the wild strain is characterized by even greater sex difference in the optimal pace for intromissions.

This paradox arises from the assumption that the male and the female experience the same intervals between intromissions. They must if mating occurs in a pair; however, the pair is not the social context in which this species usually breeds (McClintock and others, forthcoming b). Rats in the wild can survive and reproduce in large groups composed of strangers or highly genetically related individuals. During domestication, rats are bred in groups with a sex ratio of three males to four or five estrous females. Furthermore, the estrous cycles of female rats can synchronize (McClintock, 1978, in press) making it especially likely that several females will be in heat at a given time. Thus it was most likely multimale-multifemale groups, and not isolated pairs, that formed the social environment in which the mating behavior and neuroendocrine system of Norway rats evolved in the wild and were brought under domestication.

We therefore selected from the colony females that would be likely to come into estrus on the same night and placed them in the seminatural environment along with two males. By choosing to study mating in a multimale-multifemale group, we had to relinquish control over the social interactions during mating. If the Norway rat were a monogamous species, it is possible that males and females would pair off and mate with each other in a pattern similar to that of rats forced to mate in pairs. However, group mating removes the constraints of monogamous pairings, and the individuals are free to change partners in order to mate in their own preferred patterns. The male and the female no longer have to mate at the same intervals.

The rats did not remain monogamous while mating in the social context of a group. In fact, they were more than promiscuous, changing partners repeatedly during the course of copulation. The pattern of social interaction in these groups of mating rats seemed hopelessly complex at first. However, by following the interaction from the perspective of each individual, we discovered some remarkably stable features. First, the males took turns mating with all of the estrous females in the group. From the male's perspective, the mating sequence was virtually identical to the sequence seen in pairs: He had several mounts, some with intromissions, and the first of several ejaculations. At this point, the second male began mating, usually after approaching the quiescent male first. Fitting his copulation into the quiescent period of the first, the second male also completed an ejaculatory series before the first male resumed mating. Thus the ejaculatory series is a stable unit of analysis, both from the perspective of individual males and in terms of their social interactions. The number of ejaculatory series per male was increased in groups with more females. This fact suggests that the pattern of multiple ejaculatory series has evolved to allow a male to sire the litters of several females.

The females also alternated among themselves, taking turns mating with whichever male was active. However, they alternated much more frequently than the males did, after each intromission rather than after each ejaculation. The following is a short schematic of the sequence of intromissions in a group:

$$M_1F_1, \ M_1F_2, \ M_1F_3, \ M_1F_2 \rightarrow E; \ M_2F_2, \ M_2F_1, \ M_2F_3, \ M_2F_2 \rightarrow E; \ M_1F_1, \ \ldots$$

This social pattern had profound consequences for the behavioral units of analysis from the female's perspective. The ejaculatory series was not a stable unit of copulatory behavior; for example, a female could begin mating by receiving an ejaculation and then a series of intromissions, two ejaculations in a row, and finish with a few more intromissions. Other females showed completely different sequences. Despite this variability, the females still became pregnant and bore full litters. This demonstrates, then, that for the female, the intromissions that initiate sperm transport and the progestational state need not precede the ejaculation, as they must in the male. Thus, the basic unit in the organization of male sexual behavior has no meaning for the analysis of female sexual behavior. Only the total number and pacing of intromissions showed a stable pattern, not their sequence relative to an ejaculation. Thus, because females took turns mating more frequently than did the males, the females all had longer intervals between intromissions than the males. These intervals correspond to the longer temporal parameters of their neuroendocrine systems.

Mating in the social context of a group also revealed a female sexual behavior that had been eclipsed by the behavior of the male when mating took place in pairs (McClintock and others, forthcoming a). After his ejaculation, the male becomes refractory and will not mate. This quiescent behavior of the male functions to ensure that enough time will pass for the sperm of his ejaculate to be transported from the female's cervix up into the fallopian tubes for fertilization. If the male can be induced to resume mating in less than two minutes or if another male mates with the female during the first male's quiescent period, sperm transport in the female is halted immediately. Thus, in a multimale group, competition among the males can be played out in the form of sperm inhibition. However, from the female's perspective, this form of competition is risky. If she has her sperm transport inhibited but does not then receive another ejaculation, she runs the risk of achieving a progestational state from the intromissions, but doing so without conceiving. This state is called pseudopregnancy and delays the onset of estrus and its associated opportunity for pregnancy by two weeks, a delay that could substantially reduce the number of litters that a female can potentially produce in a breeding season. This risk suggests that the female has some interest in protecting her reproductive investment and remaining quiescent herself, until the sperm can be transported. In the pair, the male's postejaculatory quiescence serves this function for her. However, during group mating, the female risks pseudopregnancy if she resumes mating with a second male, immediately after receiving an ejaculation from the first. While the female had the opportunity to mate immediately, she did not take it. Instead, she entered the burrow and avoided contact with the second mating male until at least three minutes had passed. As her quiescence is slightly shorter than the male's, it is eclipsed in the pair and does not affect the pacing of mating. It is only in the social context of a group that her postejaculatory quiescence becomes evident.

## Methods for Regaining Control

In the effort to control experimental variables and create internal validity, the traditional testing environments have been designed to artificially restrict the range of behaviors and interactions that can occur to those that are the focus of a particular study. However, the focus of our research has been on the organization of behavior that allows an individual to regulate its own interactions in coordination with neuroendocrine function and the environment. Therefore our research strategy has been to move along the continuum toward the natural environment by reducing the constraints that the experimenter imposes on a behavioral interaction. In this way we have hoped to see the spontaneous behavior that an animal uses to regulate the timing of reproductive events and that is therefore more externally valid than the behavior seen under highly manipulated conditions. However, in so doing, we lost direct control over the interactions and were left with the problem of identifying loci of control and their interactive patterns without the benefit of having manipulated these variables directly. Thus we have sought to maintain control through our methods of analyzing a complex stream of behavior, rather than by simplifying the testing environment to the point that behavior is distorted.

If the immediate goal is to describe simple lawful relationships between mating behavior and neuroendocrine function, the first problem is to decide how natural the testing environment must be. The most robust conclusions will be based on the study of mating behavior in a variety of different environments that do not artificially restrict the onset or cessation of mating and that limit mating opportunities in different ways. We began by making the physical environment less restrictive and providing a larger behavioral space, the opportunity to modify that space, and the opportunity to engage in activities other than copulation.

We then studied mating in a variety of social environments. Traditionally, laboratory experiments have attempted to identify the role of the male and female during mating by creating an artificial social environment that removes one partner from the interaction. For example, when the focus of a study has been on active female sexual behavior, the male has been restrained in a neck tether (Krieger and others, 1976) or concealed until the female's bar press lifts a partition (Bermant and Westbrook, 1966). Male sexual behavior has been studied in small cages, which do not permit active solicitation by the female (McClintock and Adler, 1978). We first chose to make the social environment more natural by simply allowing both members of a pair unrestricted access to each other in a large seminatural environment. We then made the social environment more complex by adding more individuals, including those that were sexually active and those that were not. Although this left us with the task of analyzing social behavior that became increasingly complex, we generated a variety of different social contexts with which to assess the robustness of the relationship between the timing of mating behavior and the temporal parameters of neuroendocrine function.

The next step was to create from the stream of spontaneous behavior a record that was not biased by sampling problems. Such a record can be a powerful tool for discerning causal relationships between behavioral variables that have not been manipulated directly. We did this with a video system, positioned so that the entire testing environment was constantly in view and no behavioral interactions would be missed. Likewise, a time-lapse video recorder was used so that the behavioral record was continuous, without the gaps that bias the analysis of the temporal pattern of behavior (S. Altmann, in preparation). This permanent video record had many advantages: The temporal resolution and frame-by-frame analysis of the video system were precise enough to measure the temporal relationship of interactions among rats (other species might require a finer or a coarser resolution). Repeated viewings of the tapes allowed each animal, even those in the most complex social environment, to be the focal animal concurrently. With a record of all interactions from the perspective of each individual, it was possible to compare the variation among individual records to the variation arising from such group differences as sex or dominance status.

As copulation is the product of an interaction between males and females, our next task was to parcel out the relative contribution of each sex to the interaction. Thus, we could compare the temporal parameters of the male's and female's behavior to the sex-typical temporal pattern of their neuroendocrine systems. We have used several different methods for assessing the contribution of each sex to the final copulatory pattern. The first was an analysis of variance. By taking advantage of strain differences in the copulatory pattern of wild and domestic pairs, we were able to infer the relative contributions of the female and the male behavior to the pattern of copulation by studying the copulatory pattern of mixed-strain combinations. In this approach, mate choice is determined by the experimenter, but mating occurs spontaneously, regulated only by the interactions of the pair. Using this method, we concluded that the strain of the female accounted for the variance in the number of preejaculatory intromissions and that both the strain of the male and the female contributed to the variance in temporal variables such as the interval between intromissions. An analysis of variance, however, is inherently limited. It can only provide a localized analysis of the relative contributions of the male and the female under the specific environmental conditions present at the time of observation (Lewontin, 1976). In order to generalize, it is necessary to repeat the assessment in a variety of environments.

Taking a different approach, we chose to observe mating in a multimale-multifemale group where individuals would not only have unrestricted access to a partner, but where they could also select their own mates. This has the additional advantage of freeing the two sexes from the compromise imposed by mating in a pair. In order to assess the relative contributions of each sex to the temporal pattern of group mating, we analyzed the interaction of the group from the perspective of each individual and then compared the males' and the females' records. Furthermore, because intervals between temporal events usually form a negative exponential distribution (and not the normal distribution that is assumed by the more commonly used parametric analysis), we chose a log-survivor analysis. This method of analysis is extremely powerful and can provide an extraordinarily rich picture of the temporal organization of behavior. Not only is it possible to assess the rate of behavior and alterations in this rate with the passage of time, it is also possible to assess the effect of different types of social interactions on the probability of a particular behavior. This is done by statistically comparing a log-survivor plot of behavior that occurred spontaneously in one context to the log-survivor plot of behavior occurring in another. This detailed temporal information would be obliterated by an analysis that merely compared average durations or average intervals between events.

In a log-survivor analysis, the interval between two mating events is treated as a lifespan. Thus the demographic techniques that have been developed to study lifespan duration (that is, survivorship) can be applied to study the effect of different variables on the duration of the interval between behaviors (that is, its rate); see S. Altmann (in preparation), Fagen and Young (1978), Gross and Clark (1975), and McClintock and others (forthcoming b) for a detailed discussion of the use of this type of temporal analysis. The cumulative distribution of intervals is plotted semilogarithmically against time $t$ abscissa, the duration of an interval or time $t$; ordinate (log of the percentage of intervals whose lengths are greater than time $t$); see Figure 2. A log-survivor curve can be fitted either by a straight line or by a curve that is a power function. The slope of the curve at any time $t$ is proportional to the probability that the next event will occur at that time and terminate the interval between events (Fagen and Young, 1978). Thus, a log-survivor plot of intervals between events that can be fitted by a straight line indicates the probability of the next event remains constant and is independent of the passage of time since the preceding event (that is, a Poisson distribution), whereas a log-survivor plot that can be fitted by a concave curve indicates the probability of the second event decreases with the passage of time since the first, and is therefore controlled by a time-dependent process.

When the log-survivor curves of the male and the female were compared, we found again that the male's copulatory behavior is paced at a faster rate than the female's. This is particularly true if each sex takes advantage of the group context and changes partners (see the outlying curves of Figure 2). If the rats are monogamous to the extent that they mate twice in a row with the same partner, the two sexes each compromise, and their mating rates become more similar; the male mates more slowly than he otherwise would and the female mates more quickly. However, even under these conditions, the curves of the male and female are not identical. The group context allows a female to mate twice in a row with the same male when he has mated with another female in the meantime and vice versa. Therefore, even when one is comparing the temporal distribution of mating with the same partner, males mate faster than females do (McClintock and others, forthcoming c).

While this finding is robust, ideally we should assess its external validity directly by observing the behavior of the wild strain mating in the field. However, since wild Norway rats are fossorial rodents, mating at night and frequently under cover, visual observation of a complete copulatory session is difficult, if not impossible. Therefore one feasible method is to conduct a diallel cross in the laboratory using a variety of domestic strains. By doing this, Dewsbury (1975a) has inferred that domestication has decreased the intervals at which rats prefer to mate, in other words, the wild strain prefers to mate even faster. However, as his studies were conducted in a small environment,

# Figure 2. The Effect of Changing Partners on the Rate of Mating

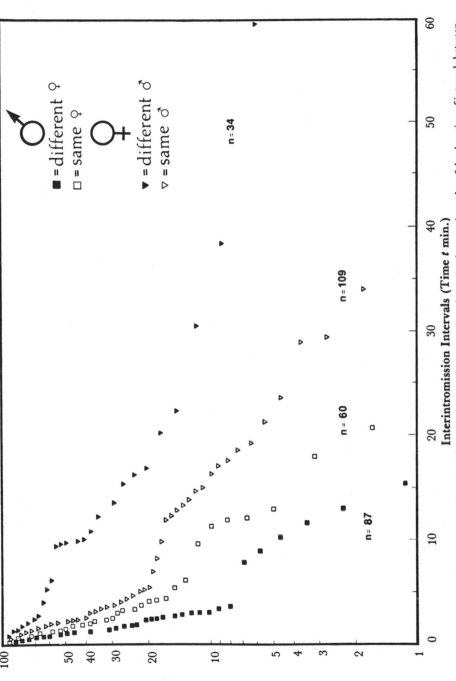

*Note:* The effect of partner changes is given from both the male and female perspective; shown is a log-survivor plot of the duration of intervals between intromissions.

[a]All four distributions differ significantly [p ≤ 0.0001, generalized (Dixon, 1979)].

which effectively removes the female's contribution to the temporal pattern, his conclusions are applicable only to a prediction about changes in the male's behavior. Another method is to directly observe the wild strain as they mate in the laboratory. Both our observations in a seminatural environment (McClintock and Adler, 1978) and those of Price (1980) in a smaller testing enclosure agree with Dewsbury's prediction, adding robustness to the finding. In order to validate the sex difference as well, and to demonstrate that it is even greater in the wild, it would also be necessary to add robustness to our finding that wild females prefer to mate more slowly than domestic females do. Thus a diallel cross should be conducted using an environment that is large and complex enough to permit female solicitation. Also, the wild strain should be observed mating in groups.

## Approximating the Natural Environment

We have used environments that contain several important features of the physical and social environment under which the Norway rat's reproductive system evolved. How do we know that we are not still studying mating in an environment that is just as bizarre and artificial as the standard laboratory testing cage? While no single laboratory environment will be identical to the range of conditions under which Norway rats evolved, it may still approximate enough features common to these environments to permit an undistorted picture of mating behavior. One of the strongest criteria for an accurate approximation of the natural environment is a match between the temporal patterns of mating behavior and the temporal parameters of the neuroendocrine system that mediate its function.

There are several such matches during group mating of domestic rats in our seminatural environment. Females pace intromissions at longer intervals than males, paralleling the sex difference in the optimal interval for stimulating neuroendocrine events in the two sexes. Furthermore, males do not resume mating until enough time has passed to allow the transport of over 90 percent of their sperm. Females take a slightly different strategy, waiting until enough time has passed to ensure some sperm transport, but then resuming mating with another male, presumably to increase their chances of having surviving offspring by having more than one male sire their litters.

Given that the behavior and the neuroendocrine system of the domestic strain meet the matching criterion under our conditions, the essential features of the natural environment of the domestic strain may simply be a multifemale-multimale group of rats breeding in a large gang cage. These are the conditions under which breeders have selected for a high reproductive rate, and thus these conditions may be the most important to include in environments used for studying mating in the domestic strain.

In our particular example of reproduction in Norway rats, the mismatch between physiology and behavior in the standard testing cage resulted from a distortion of behavior. Behavioral disruption is not always the source of a mismatch; the laboratory environment may also distort the normal timing of the neuroendocrine system, while the temporal organization of behavior remains stable. For example, in the field, female yellow baboons (*Papio cynocephalus*) remain amenorrheic for a year after giving birth if their infants survive. Once they resume their menstrual cycles, it takes an average of four months for them to conceive. Therefore they usually experience almost a two-year interval between the births of their infants (Altmann and others, 1978). Thus the neuroendocrine mechanisms that temporarily suppress the mother's menstrual cycle neatly coordinate her fertility with the amount of time that it takes to successfully raise an infant baboon to independence (Altmann, 1980). However, when female baboons reproduce in captivity, the length of their postpartum amenorrhea is reduced by a half, and the mother is physiologically capable of a second pregnancy within one year. Nevertheless, the amount of time that it takes to raise her infant to cognitive emotional and physical independence may not be reduced. Therefore, the laboratory environment alters the mother's neuroendocrine system by allowing her to become fertile at a time that is inappropriate, given the normal time and energy requirements of her first infant. In other words, the temporal conditions of neuroendocrine function and maternal behavior are disrupted.

## Conclusions

The research reported here demonstrates how the use of a simple laboratory environment can produce findings that do not generalize to other environments. Even seemingly stereotyped behavior can be distorted, as can the relationship between behavior and neuroendocrine function. By taking a naturalistic approach and including features of an animal's natural environment in the laboratory, researchers can reduce some of this distortion and permit behavior to occur in a pattern that is coordinated with neuroendocrine function. This coordination is itself an indicator that distortion by the testing environment has been minimized.

This does not mean that a natural approach can stand alone. The interpretation of behavior in a neuroendocrine context relies heavily on studies that necessitate the use of simple and controlled environments. (For example, the assessment of the temporal parameters of a neuroendocrine system may be impossible in a complex environment.)

Behavior in a more natural environment is not under the direct control of the experimenter; nonetheless, it is possible to use analytic techniques to extract simple patterns from a complicated stream of interactions. If spontaneous behavior is not artificially constrained by the laboratory environment, and if the environment contains features present during the natural selection of behavior, it is more likely to reflect the organization inherent in the animal and therefore have a simple lawful relationship with other systems.

## References

Altmann, J. *Baboon Mothers and Infants.* Cambridge, Mass.: Harvard University Press, 1980.

Altmann, J., Altmann, S. A., Hausfater, G., and McCuskey, S. A. "Life History of Yellow Baboons: Physical Development and Infant Mortality." *Primates,* 1978, *18,* 315–330.

Altmann, S. "Foraging and Nutrition of Weanling Baboons." In preparation.

Bèach, F. A. "The Snark Was a Boojum." *American Psychologist,* 1950, *5,* 115–124.

Beach, F. A., Stern, F., Carmichael, M., and Ranson, E. "Comparisons of Sexual Receptivity and Proceptivity in Female Hamsters." *Behavioral Biology,* 1976, *18,* 473–487.

Bermant, G., and Westbrook, W. H. "Peripheral Factors in the Regulation of Sexual Contact by Female Rats." *Journal of Comparative and Physiological Psychology,* 1966, *61* (2), 244–250.

Caggiula, A. R., Antelman, S. M., Chiodo, L. A., and Linelemy, C. A. "Brain DA and Sexual Behavior: Psychopharmacological and Electrophysiological Evidence for an Antagonism Between Active and Passive Components." In E. Usdin, J. Kopin, and J. Barchas (Eds.), *Catecholamines: Basic and Clinical Frontiers.* New York: Plenum Press, 1979.

Calhoun, J. B. *The Ecology and Sociology of the Norway Rat.* USPHS Publication No. 1008, 1962.

Ciaccio, L. A., Catanzaro, C., and Lisk, R. D. "Social Behavior of the Golden Hamster under Seminatural Conditions." Abstract from Animal Behavior Society meetings, New Orleans, La., 1979.

Davis, D. E. "The Relation Between Level of Population and Pregnancy of Norway Rats." *Ecology,* 1951, *32,* 459–461.

Dewsbury, D. A. "A Diallel Cross Analysis of Genetic Determinants of Copulatory Behavior in Rats." *Journal of Comparative and Physiological Psychology,* 1975a, *88* (2), 713–722.

Dewsbury, D. A. "Diversity and Adaptation in Rodent Copulatory Behavior." *Science,* December 5, 1975b, *1980,* 947–954.

Dixon, W. J. (Ed.). BMDP-79, *Biomedical Computer Programs, P Series.* Berkeley: University of California Press, 1979.

Edmonds, S., Zoloth, S. R., and Adler, N. T. "Storage of Copulatory Stimulation in the Female Rat." *Physiology and Behavior,* 1972, *8,* 161–164.

Fagen, R. M., and Young, D. Y. "Temporal Patterns of Behavior: Durations, Intervals, Latencies, and Sequences." In P. N. Colgan (Ed.), *Quantitative Ethology.* New York: Wiley, 1978.

Floody, O. R., and Pfaff, D. W. "Communication Among Hamsters by High-Frequency Acoustic Signals: III Responses Evoked by Natural and Synthetic Ultrasounds." *Journal of Comparative and Physiological Biology,* 1977, *91,* 820–829.

Gross, A. J., and Clark, V. A. *Survival Distributions.* New York: Wiley, 1975.

Hedricks, L., and McClintock, M. K. "Postpartum Estrus in the Norway Rat: Temporal Coordination of Mating Behavior and Nesting," forthcoming.

Kavenau, J. L. "Behavior: Confinement, Adaptation, and Compulsory Regimes in Laboratory Studies." *Science,* 1964, *143,* 490.

Krieger, M. S., Orr, D., and Perper, T. "Temporal Patterning of Sexual Behavior in the Female Rat." *Behavioral Biology,* 1976, *18,* 379–386.

Larsson, K. *Conditioning and Sexual Behaviour in the Male Albino Rat.* Stockholm: Almkvist and Wiksell, 1956.

Lewontin, R. C. "The Analysis of Variance and the Analysis of Causes." In N. J. Block and A. Swarkin (Eds.), *The IQ Controversy.* New York: Pantheon Books, 1976.

McClintock, M. K. "Estrous Synchrony and Its Mediation by Airborne Chemical Communication *(Rattus norvegicus).*" *Hormones and Behavior,* 1978, *10,* 264–276.

McClintock, M. K. "Behavioral Control of the Ovarian Cycle and the Function of Estrous Synchrony." *American Zoologist,* in press.

McClintock, M. K., and Adler, N. T. "The Role of the Female During Copulation in the Wild and Domestic Norway Rat *(Rattus norvegicus).*" *Behaviour,* 1978, *67,* 67–96.

McClintock, M. K., Toner, J. P., Anisko, J. J., and Adler, N. T. "The Postejaculatory Quiescent Period of Female and Male Rats. I. Demonstration During Mating in a Group." *Journal of Comparative and Physiological Psychology,* forthcoming a.

McClintock, M. K., Anisko, J. J., and Adler, N. T. "Group Mating Among Norway Rats.: I. Sex Differences in the Pattern of Copulation." *Animal Behavior,* forthcoming b.

McClintock, M. K., Anisko, J. J., and Adler, N. T. "Group Mating Among Norway Rats: II. The Social Context of Copulation: Sex Ratios, Competition and Shared Reproductive Effort." *Animal Behavior,* forthcoming c.

Price, E. O. "Sexual Behavior and Reproductive Competition in Male Wild and Domestic Norway Rats." *Animal Behavior,* 1980, *28,* 657–667.

*Martha K. McClintock is assistant professor in the Department of Behavioral Sciences, University of Chicago.*

*Contemporary personality research should lead
practicing clinicians to a renewed emphasis
on present life variables in their clients.*

# Toward a Renewed Integration of Personality Research and Clinical Practice

## Herbert M. Lefcourt
## Rod A. Martin
## Kristina Ebers

For the clinical psychologist who lives in academe there is a disquieting sense that the roles of clinical practitioner and personality researcher are independent and antagonistic. This was not always the case. From the original studies of the Office of Strategic Services (O.S.S.) candidates during World War II, a host of research findings were eventually implemented in clinical settings. Thus the names of Henry Murray, Robert White, and their collaborators became as well known in clinical psychology as in personality research. Innovative devices for assessment, such as the Thematic Apperception Test (TAT) and the Make-a-Picture Story Test, became familiar tools in the clinician's battery. So, also, was the Word Association Test, derived from Jung's procedures and the Minnesota Multiphasic Personality Inventory (MMPI) and Rorschach.

Perhaps it is the fact that contributions developed prior to the 1950s are still in vogue that is most dispiriting to the psychologist who tries to keep up with research in personality. Is it possible, one is forced to wonder, that the techniques of the 1940s were so superior that they deserved to become immutable, or have the contributions of recent personality research been so vacuous that little of clinical utility has emerged? The purpose of this chapter is to confront both of these questions, but especially the second. There is much in the literature of personality research that is of immediate relevance to the concerns of the clinician and that could supplant much of the less systematic information gathering common in clinical practice.

In a sense, many of the pursuits we recommend as valuable for the clinician have been discussed throughout the history of clinical psychology. For example, Freud pondered the manner in which individuals came to cathect particular objects and form love relationships. He thought, however, that one sacrificed self-focused libido for another when cathecting that other person. In other words, self-sacrifice was involved whenever a person became emotionally entangled with others. For Freud, however, the marvel was that persons became entangled with others at all. In fact, he maintained that men required the dread of castration to stimulate the growth of the superego. The superego in turn moderated the manner in which individuals interacted with others so as to assure more acceptable social behavior.

Other analytic writers such as Adler, Horney, and Sullivan likewise focused upon object relations. To these theorists, however, the sense of concern and involvement with others was less mysterious than was the failure to become socially engaged. No depletion of libido was assumed to occur as a price for one's involvements. Rather, as Fromm as well as some other writers asserted, the love of others could prove to be energizing.

Regardless of their shades of opinion, each of these psychoanalytic writers emphasized the importance of the relationship of people to the world around them. In psychology this concern was mirrored in the works of Kurt Lewin, who emphasized the relationships between people and their goals, that is, their objects of concern, social and otherwise. Lewin and his students strove to account for various behaviors — including persistence and shifts in attention — in terms such as levels of aspiration and proximity to goals.

Despite this congruity of concern for the examination of human involvement in real-world "objects," the practicing clinician who is forming a diagnosis more often searches for manifestations of particular pathologies, searches for signs of the relative power of particular theoretically based structures (for example, ego versus superego), or — if assessing object relations — searches unsystematically for the earlier attachments for which current persons are merely surrogates.

It is against such static notions of the patient that Mischel's original contributions (Mischel, 1968) were directed. While Mischel has been likened to Skinner in his emphasis upon the situational determinants of behavior, his contribution may be appreciated more as an attempt to recenter the clinician's focus upon real and immediate social concerns of the patient. To assess ego structure or to discriminate among varieties of pathology are not in themselves fruitless pursuits. However, if they eclipse interest in the patient's object relations — his or her concern for persons and goals in the here and now and in the future — then a major route toward a useful understanding of the patient is lost.

To state the matter sharply, Mischel has attempted to reinstate a concern for the role of the patient's present situation into the purview of the clinician: The patients' perceptions of their opportunities, their anticipations of goal fulfillment within certain circumstances, and their search for places and situations where goal attainment is more probable become likely areas of interest for clinical assessment. Recent research by Klinger (1977) indicates that a person's connectedness to current concerns is diagnostic of his or her state of well-being. That is, if a patient loses the objects of his or her commitments, there is an increasing threat of depression, which will be maximized if several such objects or incentives are lost within a brief stretch of time. Klinger's thesis suggests that involvement with incentives provides the organization for daily human activity, both action and fantasy, and that without these customary involvements humans become fragmented and despondent, a condition that could result in a search for guidance and an encounter with a clinician.

The state of a patient's relationships with significant persons and goals is of obvious importance to any practicing clinician. Often overlooked is the growing body of research findings by personality investigators; these findings could provide valuable directions for the pursuit of clinically relevant information. In the following pages we highlight some of these findings in the hope that they may lead clinicians to productive new directions.

## Current Life Events

With the introduction of a Life Events Survey, Holmes and Rahe (1967) helped to redirect much current interest into research upon the effects of events occurring in the here and now. In terms of the present discussion, the life events assessed by means of this and other similar scales may be conceptualized as shifts in an individual's relationships with valued objects. These shifts may be due to such occurrences as deaths, incapacities, and mobility. Briefly stated, these investigators found that those who experienced a great number of life changes in a relatively short span of time were more vulnerable to a variety of physical ailments. In the decade since the publication of this seminal work, numerous books, articles, and monographs have explored the impact of current and previous life experiences upon physical health, adjustment, moods, depression, anxiety, and other forms of psychopathology (see Holmes and Masuda, 1974; Paykel, 1974). Although there has been criticism of assessment methods and of some previous findings with life events scales, the point that changes in life experiences often have strong effects upon the functioning of persons has been well made. A clinician needs to know about those shifts and changes in patients' connections with their goals and in their personal relationships.

However, as most researchers concerned with life events investigations have noted, there is considerable variance in the responses of persons to similar life changes. As Johnson and Sarason (1979b) observe, life changes alone most often account for a mere 10 percent of the variance in the prediction of given stress responses. Johnson and Sarason suggest, as do Rabkin and Streuning (1976), that predictive accuracy would be enhanced by the identification of variables that moderate the deleterious effects of stressful events. It is these moderating variables, even more than the stressful events themselves, that should be of particular interest to the clinician who seeks to help individuals cope more effectively with the adverse experiences they encounter in their lives. As Andrews and his associates (1978, p. 308) point out: "The study of adverse life events is to some extent a doomsday exercise without strong public health implications, because the loss of loved ones, changes in work, and reverses of fortune are life experiences that cannot be remedied by the health services. Conversely, the study of factors mediating between stress and illness may have considerable therapeutic implications."

If clinicians become apprised of those moderators, they are better able to comprehend what qualities in patients enable them to withstand the impacts of various life stresses and what deficiencies exacerbate the stresses. The therapeutic endeavor would then be aimed at developing and mobilizing such assets, strengths, and skills. Clinicians have long sought for the chink in their patients' armor, the failing that increased the likelihood of pathological behavior. What we are proposing is merely an opposite focus—upon the strengths that can ameliorate stress-provoking situations. With this focus upon strengths rather than failings and with a redirection of concern toward present life stressors rather than earlier historical ones, we may be able to develop from the current concepts of personality research a potentially useful model for clinical psychologists.

The model is a relatively compact one. If we conceive of the life events experienced by our patients as the first variable, A, to be entered into a multiple regression equation, a range of variables that we believe to be moderators of those life events as the second set of variables, B, and the interactions between those variables, A x B, as the third set in our formulation, we should then be able to draw predictive formulas for particular pathological developments. For example, the incidence of depression or mood disturbance may be predicted from knowledge of the incidence of negative life events A, the individual's beliefs regarding his or her abilities to control important life outcomes B, and the interactions between A and B. This formulation was used successfully (Lefcourt, Miller, Ware, and Sherk, forthcoming) in the prediction of mood disturbance recorded over a month's time.

The importance of this model is that it focuses attention upon both the salient relationships between real and immediate life events and the development of emotional disturbance and upon possible mediators of that relationship. In this chapter we will attempt to describe a number of these mediators, which, if accurately assessed, should add substantially to our acumen in diagnosing the sources of manifest problems. With a detailed guide of moderator variables that have been found effective in reducing the impact of stressful life events, we may find that we are merely arriving at a clearer delineation of what has been meant by the term *ego strength*. Nevertheless, we prefer to consider the present position as being more nearly in sympathy with the position of such investigators as Jessor, Graves, Hanson, and Jessor (1968); Jessor and Jessor (1977); and Mischel (1973, 1977). Each of these investigators defines those personality characteristics (the moderators) in individuals that enable them to withstand a host of temptations and threats that could otherwise readily give rise to problems and often lead to the search for help from a clinician.

Rabkin and Struening (1976), in their critique of the literature on stressful life events, suggest that, apart from the characteristics of the stressful situation itself, moderating variables may be grouped into two broad categories: individual biological and psychological characteristics, or internal factors; and characteristics of the social support systems available to the individual, or external, interpersonal factors. It should be noted that these two types of variables are in fact interrelated: The type and extent of one's network of social support is in part determined by various cognitive and personality factors, and these are in turn influenced by one's social relationships. In the remainder of this chapter we will describe the rather encouraging research that has been reported regarding a number of moderators from both of these categories. We believe that these variables are of signal importance and that they can help us to understand what humans require to remain robust in the face of challenges.

## Individual Characteristics as Stress Moderators

Much of the earlier research on life events, following Selye's (1956) physiological model, postulates a rather direct and uncomplicated causal link between stressful life events and physical and psychological illness. However, Janis (1958) and Lazarus (1966) both point out the important role of cognitive and personality factors in producing stress reactions and suggest that stress be defined in terms of "transactions between individuals and situations, rather than of either one in isolation" (Lazarus, 1966, p. 5). In other words, whether a situation serves as a stressor or merely as a stimulus depends on various processes within the person.

Individual variation in the experiencing of stress in a particular situation may arise from differences both in appraisal processes and in coping strategies. With regard to the first of these, Sarason (1980) notes that in a given situation an individual makes appraisals both of the nature of the demands or constraints in the situation confronted and of one's available resources and skills for dealing successfully with these demands. This formulation is very similar to Lazarus' (1966) concept of primary and secondary appraisal. Differences in such appraisal processes may be due to a variety of factors, including biological and psychological threshold sensitivities, intelligence, verbal skills, morale, personality type, versatility of defenses, and breadth of previous experience (see Rabkin and Struening, 1976). The eventual impact of stressful experiences also depends on the ways in which individuals cope with them once this appraisal process has taken place. Lazarus and Launier (1978) refer to four kinds of coping strategies by individuals: (1) information seeking, (2) direct action, (3) inhibition of action, and (4) intrapsychic coping. Each of these strategies may be effective or ineffective in any given situation, and the choice of one or the other of them will similarly depend on a variety of individual factors.

A number of researchers are currently investigating these individual differences in appraisal processes and coping strategies (moderating variables), which mediate the effects of life events (for example, Antonovsky, 1974; Johnson and Sarason, 1979a). Of particular interest to the present chapter is the study recently reported by Kobasa (1979), which compared the personality characteristics of two groups of business executives who had experienced similarly large numbers of negative life events, one group of whom had subsequently become ill whereas the other had not. According to the findings of this research, the personality structure of the second group, which Kobasa has termed "hardiness," is characterized by (1) a belief that they can *control* or influence the events of their experience, (2) an ability to feel deeply involved in or *committed* to the activities of their lives, and (3) an anticipation of change as an exciting *challenge* to further development. Each of these three factors—control, commitment, and challenge—have, to varying degrees, been the subject of investigation by a number of other researchers as well.

The first characteristic of Kobasa's "hardy" individuals—a belief in their own ability to control or influence the events of their lives—is derived from the locus of control construct (see Lefcourt, 1976). Locus of control refers to the degree to which individuals generally perceive the events in their lives as being contingent upon their own actions or relatively permanent characteristics (that is, internal control), or as being relatively unrelated to their own behaviors and dependent upon external factors such as luck, fate, or powerful others (that is, external control). A number of researchers into life stress have postulated that the degree to which individuals perceive stressful events as being within or outside their own control may be an important determinant of the effects of those events (Dohrenwend and Dohrenwend, 1974; Rabkin and Struening, 1976). Numerous laboratory studies have demonstrated that subjects' responses to aversive stimuli such as electric shock and loud noise are attenuated when they perceive themselves as having some control over these stimuli, whether or not they use that control (Averill, 1973; Lefcourt, 1973). Following the model proposed by Averill, Kobasa (1979) hypothesizes that the hardy individual's sense of control involves (1) decisional control, or the ability to choose among various courses of action for handling stress; (2) cognitive control, or the ability to interpret stressful events in terms of an ongoing life plan; and (3) coping skill, or a greater repertory of suitable responses to stress.

Several recent studies provide some support for the notion that locus of control exerts a moderating effect on life stress. Johnson and Sarason (1978) found that, for subjects who scored high on Rotter's (1966) locus of control scale (externals), the number of negative life events that they reported having recently experienced was significantly correlated with measures of depression and trait anxiety, whereas no such significant relationships were found for internals. Similarly, in her study of hardiness, Kobasa (1979) found that the executives who had experienced considerable stress but who had not become ill scored significantly lower on Rotter's scale (that is, were more internal) and expressed fewer feelings of nihilism and powerlessness, as measured on an alienation scale, than did the executives who had experienced comparable stress and who had subsequently become ill.

However, recent research (Lefcourt, Miller, Ware, and Sherk, forthcoming) suggests a more complex relationship between locus of control and the effects of stressful life events. This research found that, for externals but not for internals, negative events that occurred several years previously were significantly related to enduring negative moods. However, negative events experienced within the preceding year were related to negative moods for both internals and externals. It is tentatively hypothesized that negative experiences may have an immediate impact on practically everyone, but that these effects are not as persistent for internals because of their greater goal-directedness and involvement with new pursuits.

The second characteristic of hardy individuals postulated by Kobasa is a sense of commitment to the various areas of their lives such as work, social institutions, interpersonal relationships, family, and self. She speculates that commitment to one's distinctive values, goals, and priorities provides both a sense of purpose in the face of stress, which precludes giving up on oneself and on one's social context; and an involvement with others, which furnishes an ability and a reason for turning to them for assistance in times of need. Furthermore, it is felt that commitment serves to maintain the internal balance and structure postulated by White (1959) and others (Coelho, Hamburg, and Adams, 1974) as essential for the accurate appraisal of the threat posed by life situations and for the competent handling of them. In a similar vein, Sarason (1980) hypothesizes that preoccupation with particular goals and values leads to a more adaptive task-oriented response to stress rather than maladaptive self-preoccupation. As noted earlier, the concepts of commitment to incentives, current concerns, and the deleterious consequences of disengagement from incentives have been widely explored by Klinger (1975, 1977).

The stress-buffering effect of a sense of commitment was at least partially supported in Kobasa's study. She administered to her subjects a scale that measures commitment to versus alienation from five areas of life: self, work, interpersonal relationships, family, and social institutions. The results showed only a significantly greater degree of commitment to *self* for the hardy subjects, while differences between the two groups' scores on the other four subscales, although nonsignificant, tended in the predicted direction. Further research into the moderating effects of this theoretically important construct is necessary before firm conclusions can be drawn.

Finally, Kobasa's definition of hardiness involves the "anticipation of change as an exciting challenge to further development" (1979, p. 3). She postulates that such individuals, because they value interesting experiences and are motivated for endurance, are "catalysts in their environment and are well practiced at responding to the unexpected. . . . They have a predisposition to be cognitively flexible, which allows them to integrate and effectively appraise the threat of new situations" (p. 4). Kobasa makes it clear that such a positive response to change and challenge is not an "irresponsible adventurousness."

Several other theorists and researchers have noted this tendency of some individuals to thrive on exciting and stimulating activities rather than to perceive them as stressful and shun them. Zuckerman (1974), for example, has investigated what he has termed the sensation-seeking motive, which he describes in terms of optimal level of arousal or stimulation. According to this formulation, some individuals with a high level of optimal arousal may be motivated to seek out additional stimulation because they find existing levels of environmental stimulation insufficient, whereas others with a low optimal level of arousal may find even the usual levels of stimulation uncomfortable and seek to avoid excessive arousal. Zuckerman postulates that biological factors may be involved in these individual differences. Johnson and Sarason (1979a) hypothesize that high sensation seekers, because they are better able to deal with the increased arousal brought about by life changes, may be less susceptible to the deleterious effects of such changes.

In support of this hypothesis, Kobasa found that her hardy executives, in contrast to those who became ill, expressed a significantly greater degree of vigorousness, as opposed to vegetativeness, measured on the alienation scale. Similarly, Smith, Johnson, and Sarason (1978) found recent negative life events to be significantly related to discomfort scores on a measure of neuroticism for subjects who scored low on a sensation-seeking scale, but not for high sensation seekers. These findings were replicated by Johnson, Sarason, and Siegel (1979) using anxiety and hostility scores as dependent measures.

Another concept that is closely related to sensation seeking, and one that attributes individual differences to cognitive rather than biological factors, is stimulus screening and arousability, developed by Mehrabian (1977). Rather than focusing on individuals' preferences for stimulating experiences, this construct refers to the degree of arousal or autonomic responsiveness to environmental events as a function of individual differences in "screening" versus nonselective attention to potentially arousing stimuli. Screeners are postulated by Mehrabian to impose a hierarchy of importance on various aspects of environmental events and therefore do not attend to all aspects of these events, whereas nonscreeners attend less selectively to their environment. As a result, nonscreeners tend to experience higher levels of arousal than screeners in response to these events. A study reported by Mehrabian and Ross (1977) lends support to the notion of a moderating effect of screening with the finding that, given high levels of potentially arousing life experiences, nonscreeners reported significantly more psychosomatic and nonrecurring illnesses than did screeners.

Besides the triad of control, commitment, and challenge, which have been the subject of most of the recent research, and the various closely related concepts already noted, a number of other individual difference factors may be hypothesized to play a stress-buffering role. One example of these is sense of humor. Freud (1959, 1960) described humor, which he distinguished from wit and the comic, as the highest form of the defense mechanisms, a means of turning an event that would otherwise cause suffering into one of less significance and of gaining pleasure despite the disturbing and painful experiences of life. A number of clinicians have noted the therapeutic effects provided by a judicious use of humor in psychotherapy. In this regard, Mindess (1971, p. 214) states, "Deep, genuine humor—the humor that deserves to be called therapeutic, that can be instrumental in our lives—extends beyond jokes, beyond wit, beyond laughter itself to a peculiar frame of mind. It is an inner condition, a stance, a point of view, or in the largest sense an attitude to life."

Humor, then, may involve a particular cognitive appraisal style—an ability to gain a different and unusual perspective on even the undesirable experiences of life. Humor may also serve to enhance social relationships and the stress-buffering support that these relationships provide. In recent studies we found that subjects who laughed and smiled more frequently in an interview were rated by their friends as having a closer relationship with them. Laughter and the experience of humor may also exert a physiological effect on various health mechanisms in the body. The therapeutic effects of humor and laughter were recently supported by Cousins' (1979) autobiographical account of the role of humor in his personal triumph over a rare and serious disease.

## Interpersonal Moderating Variables

We have briefly surveyed some of the current evidence concerning the stress-moderating effects of a number of personality variables. We now turn to research into the role played by interpersonal factors. A growing body of empirical evidence suggests that social support may be of profound importance in moderating the negative impact of stressful life changes (Silver and Wortman, 1981). Social support refers to an individual's access to interpersonal resources, particularly in times of need. Such interpersonal resources might be described as either proximal, such as the perception of a supportive spouse, family members, colleague or neighbor; or distal, such as the perception of belonging to a reciprocating social network (for example, the extended family, community, social groups, or institutions).

A number of studies demonstrate that perceived social support mitigates the deleterious consequences to physical health when people experience stressful life changes. For example, in one of the earliest of these studies, Nuckolls, Cassel, and Kaplan (1972) investigated the relationship of life stress and social support to pregnancy and birth complications. Although attitudinal measures were included, their psychosocial assets scale can be regarded essentially as a composite index of social support. Neither life stress nor social support by themselves reliably predicted the frequency of pregnancy or birth complications. However, when they considered the variables conjointly, they found that women who experienced high levels of stress prior to and during pregnancy and who perceived themselves as having few social resources were three times more likely to experience complications as compared to similarly stressed women who reported having adequate social resources.

In a similar vein, de Araujo, Van Arsdel, Holmes, and Dudley (1973) demonstrated that highly stressed adult asthmatics with low levels of social support required three to four times as much adrenocorticosteroid medication to control their symptoms as did similarly stressed asthmatics with high levels of social support. Medalie and Goldbourt (1976) provided further corroborative evidence. In a five-year study of 10,000 Israeli men, these researchers found that even in the presence of high-risk factors such as age (forty years and over), increased serum cholesterol levels, electrocardiographic abnormalities, and high anxiety, the wife's demonstration of love and support to her husband reduced the risk of developing angina pectoris from 93 to 52 per 1,000 (compare an average annual incidence of 5.7 per 1,000).

The stress-buffering effects of social support have also been demonstrated in the development of psychiatric as well as physiological symptoms. For example, Eaton (1978), pursuing an earlier research project (Myers, Lindenthal, Pepper, and Ostrander, 1972), demonstrated that highly stressed individuals who were unmarried or lived alone were more likely to develop psychiatric symptoms than similarly stressed individuals who were married or lived with another person. The study by Brown, Bhrolchain, and Harris (1975) yielded similar results with regard to depression. They found that women who had recently experienced severe life stress and lacked a close, confiding relationship were ten times more likely to be depressed than women who had experienced similar levels of stress and who had a confidant. Other types of social support were not found to provide sufficient protection against the development of depression as a consequence of severe life stress.

In a recent review of the literature on coping with undesirable life events, Silver and Wortman (1981) cite a number of studies that corroborate the notion that adequate social support mitigates the deleterious consequences to health status in adjusting to a wide variety of stressful events such as job loss, physical disability, terminal illness, surgery, bereavement, and rape. However, not all studies demonstrate the moderating effect of social support in the relationship of life stress to health impairment (Andrews and others, 1978).

Despite these inconsistent findings, the level of consensus concerning the stress-moderating effects of social support is noteworthy. Such consensus is particularly remarkable given the multiplicity of operational definitions of social support, definitions ranging from the delineation of marital status to an assessment of the quality of personal social networks. The development of reliable, validated instruments of measurement is of major concern in the advancement of this research area. However, despite the calls for such instruments (Dean and Lin, 1977; Johnson and Sarason, 1979a), there has been only moderate progress in this direction (see Miller and Lefcourt, 1979).

More recently researchers have begun to refine the social support construct by investigating its components. Silver and Wortman (1981) suggest that social support may involve at least five functions that aid effective adjustment to life stress: (1) the conveyance of positive feelings such as the expression that one is cared for, loved, esteemed and valued (Cobb, 1976; note also the concept of unconditional positive regard and acceptance developed by Rogers, 1961); (2) the validation of the stressed individual's feelings and cognitions as normative; (3) the encouragement of an open expression of feelings and cognitions; (4) the provision of material aid; and (5) the conveyance of information about one's belongingness to a mutually reciprocating social network (Cobb, 1976).

Research endeavors are not only being directed toward further corroborating the moderating effect of social support across a variety of life stressors and toward identifying the component functions of this construct. In addition, another line of research focuses upon delimiting the role and extent of the stress-buffering effect of social support with respect to the supported and supporting individuals' personalities and commitments. Such considerations are demanded by the recognition that social support, however it may be operationalized, represents a dynamic transactional process set within a time perspective peculiar to the individuals concerned. For example, let us reconsider Medalie and Goldbourt's (1976) simple measure of social support as the response to the dichotomously rated question, "Does your wife show you her love?" In this study, Medalie and Goldbourt found that the wife's demonstration of love and support significantly reduced the risk of her husband's developing angina pectoris even in the presence of other high-risk factors. One might conjecture that a wife's expression of love and support depends upon both her ability and willingness to communicate such information which, in turn, depends upon her husband's (and others') ability and willingness to acknowledge her conveyance of such information. The particular pattern of communication develops over numerous interactions between the spouses and with significant others. Given sensitive measuring instruments, a researcher might be able to detect across time the natural variance inherent in the particular pattern of social support for a given sample of intimate partners.

In a series of studies Lefcourt and associates (1979) investigated various factors that might be relevant to the understanding of social competence and tendencies toward self-disclosure. These researchers demonstrated that female undergraduates who attributed success in affiliation (friendship) to their own efforts demonstrated a significantly increased amount of self-disclosure in a dyadic, same-sex interaction as the set topics became more personal. The results for males, although not statistically significant, tended in the same direction. This finding indicates that women who are internal in terms of locus of control for affiliation may well be the most facile at soliciting social support when stressed. Moreover, one might conjecture that these women are the ones who most need the type of social support that facilitates the ventilation of feelings and attitudes.

A subsequent study by these same authors focused on cues that facilitate the verbal productivity of speakers engaged in a three-minute, same-sex dyadic interaction. The topic of discussion was aspects of themselves that the speakers would like to change. The results showed that the duration of speech and the speakers' ratings of comfort, acceptance, and listener interest were all positively related to the listeners' attribution of affiliation success to ability and effort. In other words, people who are internal in terms of affiliation locus of control seem to be the best listeners. In terms of delineating specific social support functions, these findings suggest that one effective match would be a person inclined toward self-disclosure when stressed (a female internal for affiliation locus of control) and an interested, accepting listener (a male internal for affiliation locus of control).

Apart from the factors that facilitate social competence and self-disclosure, the meaning of social support seems to vary as a function of the stressed individual's dominant needs. McClelland (1975, 1979) compared the effects of life stress for male college students rated according to their needs for power and affiliation. Need for power was defined as a heightened tendency to deal with others in an aggressive or assertive manner. It was found that the students' health depended largely on whether the situational stressor challenged their dominant motive dispositions. To illustrate, males with dominant power motives were much more likely to suffer impaired health when they experienced situational challenges to their power status than when the stress related to other less dominant needs, such as affiliation. McClelland concluded that when the stress is related to the dominant motive disposition in the individual, it is more likely to be associated with illness. These findings suggest that the function of social support varies with stress as it relates to the hierarchy of needs of the stressed individual. One might speculate that an individual who experiences frustration of affiliation needs may require reassurance that he or she is cared for, loved, and valued. However, the person who experiences frustration of achievement needs may require encouragement to ventilate his or her feelings and attributions, a reminder of his or her past accomplishments and potential for achievement, or assistance in developing better methods of ensuring achievement success.

Our present understanding of the important role of social support is clearly far from comprehensive and definitive. Nevertheless, Silver and Wortman's (1981) review of the theoretical and empirical literature on coping with undesirable life events indicates that a number of promising research programs are currently in progress.

## Conclusion

In keeping with the theme of this volume, we have focused upon research that should affect the manner in which clinical psychologists cope with the real-life problems of their clients. Although not all of the research described can be strictly identified as laboratory investigation, the central issue remains the same — there is a need to bridge the findings of research to their applications in the real world.

As we have noted in this chapter, a range of personal and social factors can be seen as moderator variables. Persons who enjoy closeness with others and have a range of social supports at their disposal will respond more successfully to stressful life events. Likewise, those who believe in their own efficacy, who are more committed to their incentives, who are more responsive to challenges with action, and who remain hopeful in their pursuit of goals are less apt to display the deleterious effects of stress, which often bring persons to a clinician's attention. It is our hope that clinical psychologists may come to view these constructs as assessable variables that should be examined during clinical interactions. Such assessed characteristics would lend themselves quite readily to therapeutic goals and procedures, which are often ignored in the process of diagnostic testing.

How could one go about assessing some of the constructs mentioned above? There is always the easily ascertained demographic information from which, for example, social supports could be assessed. Interviews, likewise, can provide much information about depth of intimacy, opportunity for ventilation, beliefs regarding efficacy, and so on. It is also possible to construct tests, such as incomplete sentence blanks and TAT-like procedures, to better sample the current involvements of clients. It would seem desirable to have a file of TAT-like pictures that focus upon life problems of persons grouped by sex, age, socioeconomic class, and so on. One should then be able to pull out a set of cards depicting, for example, the likely current problems of a sixty-year-old man from a comfortable middle-class background. Pictures of a man confronting the potential boredom of retirement, experiencing the fear of waning sexual interests, fearing his death or the death of his spouse, and so on, are more likely to elicit useful information than the standardized set of pictures in the current TAT battery.

Similarly, an incomplete sentences test pertinent to persons' likely current concerns at their given ages and stages of life would seem more useful than a standard form. Thus, a test for a teenage youth should include sentence stems that elicit information about the state of his friendships with peers, struggles in school, and dating relationships. However, the test for a thirty-year-old housewife might contain sentence stems that address marriage, parenting, and the relationship with her spouse.

In each of these examples our purpose is to suggest that the nature of clients' current object relations may be a productive area for clinicians to explore in their attempts to assess the sources of their clients' difficulties. Given the model of stressors/moderator variables/outcomes, it is possible that we can create a stronger bond between the concerns of personality researchers and those of clinical psychologists—between the laboratory and real life.

## References

Andrews, G., Tennant, C., Hewson, D. M., and Vaillant, G. E. "Life Event Stress, Social Support, Coping Style, and Risk of Psychological Impairment." *Journal of Nervous and Mental Disease,* 1978, *166,* 307–316.

Antonovsky, A. "Conceptual and Methodological Problems in the Study of Resistance Resources and Stressful Life Events." In B. S. Dohrenwend and B. P. Dohrenwend (Eds.), *Stressful Life Events: Their Nature and Effects.* New York: Wiley, 1974.

Averill, J. R. "Personal Control over Aversive Stimuli and Its Relationship to Stress." *Psychological Bulletin,* 1973, *80,* 286-303.

Brown, G. W., Bhrolchain, M. N., and Harris, T. "Social Class and Psychiatric Disturbance Among Women in an Urban Population." *Sociology,* 1975, *5,* 225-254.

Cobb, S. "Presidential Address: Social Support as a Moderator of Life Stress." *Psychosomatic Medicine,* 1976, *38.* 300-314.

Coelho, G., Hamburg, D. A., and Adams, J. E. (Eds.). *Coping and Adaptation.* New York: Basic Books, 1974.

Cousins, N. *Anatomy of an Illness.* New York: Norton, 1979.

de Araujo, G., Van Arsdel, P. P., Holmes, T. H., and Dudley, D. L. "Life Change, Coping Ability, and Chronic Intrinsic Asthma." *Journal of Psychosomatic Research,* 1973, *17,* 359-363.

Dean, A., and Lin, N. "The Stress-Buffering Role of Social Support: Problems and Prospects for Systematic Investigation." *Journal of Nervous and Mental Disease,* 1977, *165,* 403-417.

Dohrenwend, B. S., and Dohrenwend, B. P. "Overview and Prospects for Research on Stressful Life Events." In B. S. Dohrenwend and B. P. Dohrenwend (Eds.), *Stressful Life Events: Their Nature and Effects.* New York: Wiley, 1974.

Eaton, N. W. "Life Events, Social Supports, and Psychiatric Symptoms: A Reanalysis of the New Haven Data." *Journal of Health and Social Behavior,* 1978, *19,* 230-234.

Freud, S. "Humor." In J. Strachey (Ed.), *Sigmund Freud: Collected Papers.* Vol. 5. New York: Basic Books, 1959.

Freud, S. *Jokes and Their Relation to the Unconscious.* New York: Norton, 1960.

Holmes, T. H., and Masuda, M. "Life Changes and Illness Susceptibility." In B. S. Dohrenwend and B. P. Dohrenwend (Eds.), *Stressful Life Events: Their Nature and Effects.* New York: Wiley, 1974.

Holmes, T. H., and Rahe, R. H. "The Social Readjustment Rating Scale." *Journal of Psychosomatic Research,* 1967, *11,* 213-218.

Janis, I. *Psychological Stress.* New York: Wiley, 1958.

Jessor, R., Graves, T. D., Hanson, R. C., and Jessor, S. *Society, Personality, and Deviant Behavior.* New York: Holt, Rinehart and Winston, 1968.

Jessor, R., and Jessor, S. *Problem Behavior and Psychosocial Development.* New York: Academic Press, 1977.

Johnson, J. H., and Sarason, I. G. "Life Stress, Depression, and Anxiety: Internal-External Control as a Moderator Variable." *Journal of Psychosomatic Research,* 1978, *22,* 205-208.

Johnson, J. H., and Sarason, I. G. "Moderator Variables in Life Stress Research." In I. G. Sarason and C. D. Spielberger (Eds.), *Stress and Anxiety.* Vol. 6. Washington, D.C.: Hemisphere, 1979a.

Johnson, J. H., and Sarason, I. G. "Recent Developments in Research on Life Stress." In V. Hamilton and D. M. Warburton (Eds.), *Human Stress and Cognition: An Information Processing Approach.* New York: Wiley, 1979b.

Johnson, J. H., Sarason, I. G., and Siegel, J. M. "Arousal Seeking as a Moderator of Life Stress." *Perceptual and Motor Skills,* 1979, *49,* 665-666.

Klinger, E. "Consequences of Commitment to and Disengagement from Incentives." *Psychological Review,* 1975, *82,* 1-25.

Klinger, E. *Meaning and Void.* Minneapolis: University of Minnesota Press, 1977.

Kobasa, S. C. "Stressful Life Events, Personality, and Health: An Inquiry into Hardiness." *Journal of Personality and Social Psychology,* 1979, *37,* 1-11.

Lazarus, R. S. *Psychological Stress and the Coping Process.* New York: McGraw-Hill, 1966.

Lazarus, R. S., and Launier, R. "Stress-Related Transactions Between Person and Environment." In L. A. Pervin and M. Lewis (Eds.), *Perspectives in Interactional Psychology*. New York: Plenum Press, 1978.

Lefcourt, H. M. "The Function of the Illusions of Control and Freedom." *American Psychologist*, 1973, *28*, 417–425.

Lefcourt, H. M. *Locus of Control: Current Trends in Theory and Research*. Hillsdale, N.J.: Erlbaum, 1976.

Lefcourt, H. M., Miller, R. S., Ware, E. E., and Sherk, D. "Locus of Control as a Modifier of the Relationship Between Stressors and Moods." *Journal of Personality and Social Psychology*, forthcoming.

Lefcourt, H. M., von Baeyer, C. L., Ware, E. E., and Cox, D. J. "The Multidimensional–Multiattributional Causality Control Scale." *Canadian Journal of Behavioral Science*, 1979, *11*, 286–304.

McClelland, D. C. *Power: The Inner Experience*. New York: Irvington-Halsted-Wiley, 1975.

McClelland, D. C. "Inhibited Power Motivation and High Blood Pressure in Men." *Journal of Abnormal Psychology*, 1979, *88*, 182–190.

Medalie, J. H., and Goldbourt, U. "Angina Pectoris Among 10,000 Men: Psychosocial and Other Risk Factors as Evidenced by a Multivariate Analysis of a Five-Year Incidence Study." *American Journal of Medicine*, 1976, *60*, 910–921.

Mehrabian, A. "Individual Differences in Stimulus Screening and Arousability." *Journal of Personality*, 1977, *46*, 237–250.

Mehrabian, A., and Ross, M. "Quality of Life Change and Individual Differences in Stimulus Screening in Relation to Incidence of Illness." *Psychological Reports*, 1977, *41*, 267–278.

Miller, R. S., and Lefcourt, H. M. "The Stress-Buffering Function of Social Intimacy." Unpublished manuscript, University of Waterloo, Ontario, 1979.

Mindess, H. *Laughter and Liberation*. Los Angeles: Nash, 1971.

Mischel, W. *Personality and Assessment*. New York: Wiley, 1968.

Mischel, W. "Toward a Cognitive Social Learning Reconceptualization of Personality." *Psychological Review*, 1973, *80*, 252–283.

Mischel, W. "On the Future of Personality Measurement." *American Psychologist*, 1977, *32*, 246–254.

Myers, J. K., Lindenthal, J. J., Pepper, M. P., and Ostrander, D. R. "Life Events and Mental Status: A Longitudinal Study." *Journal of Health and Social Behavior*, 1972, *13*, 398.

Nuckolls, K. B., Cassel, J., and Kaplan, B. H. "Psychosocial Assets, Life Crisis, and the Prognosis of Pregnancy." *American Journal of Epidemiology*, 1972, *95*, 431–441.

Paykel, E. S. "Life Stress and Psychiatric Disorder: Applications of the Clinical Approach." In B. S. Dohrenwend and B. P. Dohrenwend (Eds.), *Stressful Life Events: Their Nature and Effects*. New York: Wiley, 1974.

Rabkin, J. G., and Struening, E. L. "Life Events, Stress, and Illness." *Science*, 1976, *194*, 1013–1020.

Rogers, C. R. *On Becoming a Person*. Boston: Houghton Mifflin, 1961.

Rotter, J. B. "Generalized Expectancies for Internal Versus External Control of Reinforcement." *Psychological Monographs*, 1966, *80*, (entire issue).

Sarason, I. G. "Life Stress, Self-Preoccupation, and Social Supports." In I. G. Sarason and C. D. Spielberger (Eds.), *Stress and Anxiety*. Vol. 7. Washington, D.C.: Hemisphere, 1980.

Selye, H. *The Stress of Life*. New York: McGraw-Hill, 1956.

Silver, R. L., and Wortman, C. B. "Coping with Undesirable Life Events." In J. Garber and M. E. P. Seligman (Eds.), *Human Helplessness: Theory and Application*. New York: Academic Press, 1981.

Smith, R. E., Johnson, J. H., and Sarason, I. G. "Life Change, the Sensation-Seeking Motive, and Psychological Distress." *Journal of Consulting and Clinical Psychology,* 1978, *46,* 348–349.

White, R. W. "Motivation Reconsidered: The Concept of Competence." *Psychological Review,* 1959, *66,* 297–333.

Zuckerman, M. "The Sensation-Seeking Motive." In B. Maher (Ed.), *Progress in Experimental Personality Research.* Vol. 7. New York: Academic Press, 1974.

*Herbert M. Lefcourt is professor of psychology, University of Waterloo, Ontario.*

*Rod A. Martin and Kristina Ebers are graduate students in the Department of Psychology, University of Waterloo, Ontario.*

*Research on laboratory–life generalizability has focused too*
*narrowly on the data of individual experiments and their*
*specific naturalistic counterparts.*

# Is It Possible to Measure Generalizability from Laboratory to Life, and Is It Really That Important?

## John Jung

In recent years there has been increasing concern about the issue of the generalizability of findings between laboratory experiments and their counterparts in natural settings. No experiment using human subjects is exempt from this type of evaluation. Perhaps part of this increased concern has been due to the pressure to justify research by demonstrating its relevance and practical application. Development of naturalistic research methods has also increased the availability of comparable studies that were done in the two settings. When discrepancies were noted between the laboratory and real-life versions, awareness and concern about generalizability were increased.

Despite this heightened attention to the issue, very little of consequence has been done. If Mark Twain were alive, he might say that everyone is talking about generalizability but no one is doing very much about it. I might add that the little being done about it may in fact be misleading. Much of this activity involves polemical arguments, speculations, and post hoc comparisons, but there is little in the way of sound methodology available to measure the extent to which generalizability exists between laboratory and life. As Tunnell (1977) observes, the external validity of experiments is often subjective and unquantifiable.

One argument of this chapter is that the typical procedures used to draw inferences about the generalizability of laboratory studies are so grossly confounded that if an experiment using such a design were submitted for publication, it would be immediately rejected. Experimenters who wish to make inferences about the effects of any variable other than that of laboratory versus real-life setting realize the necessity of manipulating it as an independent variable in an experiment that controls all other variables. Yet these same researchers adopt a much less stringent criterion for drawing conclusions about the effects of setting. They tend to ignore other differences that may exist between a real-life phenomenon and its laboratory analogue and attribute any differences in findings, without hesitation, to the lack of external validity of the laboratory version.

As shown in Table 1, there are a number of major differences between laboratory and natural setting studies, as they are typically conducted, that are not intrinsic to the nature of the settings. For example, most laboratory studies on any given topic typically have used college students as subjects, while natural setting studies have drawn subjects from a wide variety of sources. Yet this difference is not dictated by the setting—there is no inherent connection between this subject profile and type of setting. The existence of many such incidental differences in studies done on the same topic in the two settings jeopardizes any sound inferences about the extent of the effect of setting in creating differences in results.

**Table 1. Major Differences Between Laboratory and Life Settings Which May Confound Inferences About Generalizability**

| Potential Confounding Variable | Laboratory Setting | |
|---|---|---|
| | Laboratory | Natural |
| Type of Subjects | College Psychology Students | Varies Widely With Topic |
| Method of Assignment to Treatments | Random | Self-selection |
| Duration of Exposure to Treatment | Brief, Less Than One Hour | Varies, But Can Be Months, Years |
| Type of Dependent Variables | Quantifiable, Objective, Unidimensional | Often Subjective, Global, Multidimensional |

## How Inferences About Generalizability Are Typically Made

A frequent problem in the issue of generalizability from laboratory to life is discrepancy in the findings of two analogous studies — one in the laboratory and one in a naturalistic setting. The exact form of the real-life evidence can vary widely and may involve surveys, natural observations, or even controlled field experiments. Usually evidence from the natural setting will be taken as the criterion against which the laboratory study is evaluated. Willems and Raush (1969) question this conception and suggest that it is inadequate, even though it seems to have strong support (for example, Silverman, 1977).

As an example, let us look at a well-known experiment by Darley and Latané (1968) that involved an examination of the effect of the number of bystanders on the likelihood that a subject would seek aid for a person in an emergency. In this laboratory experiment, subjects thought they were interacting with either one or four other subjects. They communicated with each other through an intercom and could not see the other subjects, who, in fact, did not exist. At one point, the subject heard another subject experience an apparent epileptic seizure.

How long would it take solo subjects to seek assistance? The results showed that when the subjects thought they were the only witness to the emergency they were quicker to seek aid than when they thought there were other people who also could have sought aid.

Piliavin, Rodin, and Piliavin (1969), however, questioned the generalizability of this laboratory experiment. Their naturalistic replication in a New York subway involved a staged emergency in which a male victim fell to the floor of a subway car in apparent distress. The staged emergency elicited an abundance of assistance even when there were as many as seven other bystanders. It seems clear that the Darley and Latané results did not apply to this real-life situation.

Can we assume, however, that the type of setting was the major factor responsible for the different results? There were a number of other variables in the two studies, such as the fact that the subway situation involved direct observation of the victim as well as face-to-face confrontation with the other witnesses, unlike the laboratory study. Furthermore, in the real-life experiment there was no way to escape the situation until the train reached the next station.

Despite the impossibility of identifying exactly which factor accounts for the different results in the laboratory and life studies in this example, these studies are often cited as another example of the lack of generalizability of laboratory experiments. This faulty reasoning is common and by no means limited to individual laboratory experiments. Such reasoning is also found in larger bodies of research.

Many years ago Hovland (1959) reviewed the literature and pointed out disparities in the conclusions drawn from laboratory and field studies about the effectiveness of persuasive communications. Whereas correlations between attitude change and certain aspects of the communications showed little or no relationship in real life, the laboratory experiments typically produced impressive correlations.

In his analysis, Hovland noted a number of important differences in the details of the laboratory and real-life studies. Among them were the type of audience, type of topic, and type of communicator. In addition, the laboratory experiments involved the requirement that the subjects to receive the communication be selected by a method that did not consider their attitude toward the topic communicated, whereas there was high degree of self-selection among natural audiences in determining who became exposed to the communications. We can consider each of these factors as a potential source of confounding for any conclusions that might be drawn about the effect of the settings themselves. The differences in variables were not inherent distinguishing features of the laboratory and natural settings, and it may be that any differences in results were entirely or at least partially due to their influence.

Another point of comparison between naturalistic and laboratory studies can be drawn from the evaluation of the effects of perceived and real reactions of others on an individual's self-concept (Shrauger and Schoeneman, 1979). According to the symbolic interactionist view (Cooley, 1902; Mead, 1934), a person's self-concept is, to a large extent, a reflection of how other people react to that individual, or at least the person's perceptions of these reactions. Naturalistic correlational studies involved comparisons of the subjects' own self-concepts and the real or perceived views of other persons. Laboratory studies employed fake or contrived reports of test scores or subjective reports prepared by the experimenter, which results were made available to the subject. Shrauger and Schoeneman's review of the literature led them to conclude that there was low generalizability between the laboratory and real-life situations. Whereas the laboratory experiments showed strong influences on self-concept of feedback from others, the real-life studies failed to support this relationship.

Again, we must raise the question of whether the major difference between the two settings is setting, per se. Potential confounding factors include the fact that most of the laboratory studies used younger subjects who, as Shrauger and Schoeneman suggest, may be more susceptible to social influence. Another difference is the fact that the feedback from others can sometimes be deliberately sought after or avoided by an individual.

## Errors of Post Hoc Tests of Generalizability

Drawing on the logic of statistical hypothesis testing, we can say there are two types of errors one can make when drawing conclusions about the generalizability from laboratory to life. One can claim that the two settings yield different results when in fact the results are similar. This Type I error occurs when one mistakenly rejects the null hypothesis. Unlike the case in statistical inference, however, it is not due to random fluctuation but to the existence of systematically confounded comparisons. When differences between two studies exist in factors other than setting, per se, one or more of these other factors may be responsible for creating the difference in results.

Suppose we compare the effect of setting on helping behavior and find that people help those in need in our naturalistic study but not in our laboratory version. Suppose also that in real life the helpers expected the beneficiary to reciprocate or return the favor at some later date whereas this expectation did not exist in the laboratory analogue. Due to the confounded comparison we would conclude that setting makes a difference, but if we could equate the expectations in the two settings we might very well find no difference due to setting and conclude that there is high generalizability.

A Type II error in making conclusions about generalizability involves the conclusion that there is no difference in results due to setting when there really is. This error is also possibly due to confounded comparisons. If the confounding variable has an effect on behavior opposite to the effect of setting, it may mask the influence of setting so that we conclude erroneously that setting has no effect. For example, laboratory and naturalistic studies of the effects of televised violence have generally agreed that it may increase aggressive behavior (Bandura, 1973). Thus, it would appear that there is high generalizability, but upon closer analysis it may turn out to be coincidental because the underlying processes are not the same in the two studies. In the laboratory experiments, subjects are randomly assigned to view certain programs so that causal inferences may be made about whether the viewing causes the aggressive behavior. In contrast, in real life there is apt to be a self-selection process. It may be that those who choose to watch more aggressive fare may already be more aggressive than those who prefer to watch nonaggressive programs (Stein, Friedrich, and Vondracek, 1972). Thus, the similarity of results between the two settings may be more apparent than real. The evaluation of type of setting is jeopardized by the confounding effect of two different methods of assigning the content to be viewed.

The problem is: How do we know, in a given situation, whether we are committing either type of error? Unless we control all other variables while varying only the factor of setting, we are as likely to be guilty of one type as the other.

Which error is the more serious: In statistical inference, the more cautious approach is to avoid Type I errors. In the case of generalizability, however, Type II errors are more serious because we may assume there is no difference as a function of setting and conclude that generalizability is high when it is really low. The Type I error, where we falsely argue there is no generalizability, may lead to errors of omission in failures to apply potentially useful findings. The Type II error, however, may lead to the unwarranted application of laboratory data to real-life situations, which is an error of commission.

How might we solve this problem of identifying the extent of generalizability across settings? Ideally, we should use the same method we use in dealing with problems of generalizability across other factors, such as subjects, tasks, or dependent measures. We include the factor in question as a separate independent variable and check to see whether the effects of other variables hold up across the new variable or whether interactions are involved. By designing a factorial experiment in which one factor is setting, we can empirically establish that generalizability of results exists if there is no interaction of the effect with the setting. This direct solution has apparently never been used! This situation should not be too surprising since the cost of time, effort, and resources necessary to conduct parallel laboratory-life comparisons would be overwhelming.

## Conceptual Problems

Most discussions of generalizability seem to imply that a given laboratory experiment can be compared against the yardstick represented by a natural setting counterpart. A major limitation of this concept is that there are many natural settings, not just one, in which one might legitimately attempt to replicate a laboratory experiment. Suppose we conduct a laboratory experiment to assess the effects of situational anxiety on the memorization of pairs of nonsense syllables and find that high anxiety leads to better performance. Which of the following natural settings is the best in which to test the generalizability of the laboratory results: memorizing French vocabulary and English equivalents, memorizing the proper pronounciation of the words, or memorizing pairs of words from two unknown foreign languages? Any of these situations might be regarded, on the surface, to be a better criterion than say, learning a motor skill or learning how to understand statistics. It becomes more difficult, however, to determine which of the former set of tasks is most similar to the laboratory task.

In other words, there is no single natural setting counterpart of a given experiment, but instead, there are many parallel situations. The effect of anxiety in memorization of nonsense syllables may yield effects generalizable to one natural setting but not to other equally plausible natural settings. Obviously we need some objective basis for deciding which natural setting counterpart is most appropriate if we are to be able to make valid conclusions about generalizability.

Even if we could agree on which natural setting criterion to use for a given experiment, how much generalizability would we need to feel satisfied?

Total generalizability is unrealistic, of course, but how *little* generalizability can we accept? This question may be of academic interest only since we have no objective method for quantifying this dimension.

Perhaps we really do not expect generalizability to be very high at all. After all, any given experiment can only look at a few of the many factors which affect any complex real-life situation. The experiment is an analytical tool designed to look at the effects of one or a few factors *as if* the other factors did not exist or matter. As we shall see later, overconcern with generalizability may be counterproductive.

## Why Generalizability Must Be Less Than Perfect

Any human laboratory experiment is not only a research situation but also a social interaction. Since subjects are usually voluntary participants who are aware that their behavior is being observed, there is some inevitable distortion of their typical behavior. This reactive aspect of experiments may be minimized by such means as the use of highly involving tasks, but it is still usually present to an extent sufficient to reduce laboratory to life generalizability.

Although there is some disagreement (Weber and Cook, 1972) as to the nature of the primary roles or attitudinal sets that subjects assume while they participate in experiments, it is generally acknowledged that most subjects are highly apprehensive and are concerned either about looking good or about trying to behave in ways they think are expected by the experimenter. Both motives will alter the behavior from that which might occur in everyday life. The work of Rosenthal and his associates (1976) points out the influence of experimenter expectancies on the behavior of subjects in laboratory experiments. Although increased awareness of this tendency may have served to reduce the incidence of this factor in psychological research, it can, when it occurs, produce laboratory to life discrepancies in results.

We cannot assume that subjects perceive the experimental situation in the way intended by the experimenter. The meaning the subject attaches to the experimental task is a matter for empirical determination. The research of Orne (1970) on demand characteristics is important since it demonstrates the necessity of determining the extent to which the subject's perception of the situation matches the one intended by the experimenter. If there is a discrepancy, it is hardly surprising when the experimental results disagree with observations based on natural settings.

We cannot assume that the operational definitions devised by the experimenter are valid embodiments of the real-life phenomena to be represented. Sometimes ethical constraints prevent the use of realistic conditions in the laboratory. In other instances there may be poor conceptual thinking in creating the laboratory analogue. For example, Cartwright (1971) points out the lack of measurement of the actual content of group discussions in most research on the risky shift (Kogan and Wallach, 1964). Changes in the pre- and postgroup discussion risk preference levels are taken to reflect group influences on individual levels of risk taking in these studies. But Cartwright argues that we have no compelling evidence that subjects are actually making decisions about risk at all. Examination of the content of the group discussions would have shed some light on this issue. If Cartwright is correct, these studies are not valid measures of risk taking and there should, of course, be little generalizability between laboratory and natural setting results.

All of these factors contribute to the reduction of generalizability between laboratory and life. Factors which are nevertheless able to generate apparently high correspondences between the two situations must be highly potent, indeed. Since generalizability must be lower than perfect, unless we have some level of acceptable generalizability specified in advance it does little good to criticize a laboratory study on this ground. We need to know how much generalizability is acceptable for a given purpose and contrast the obtained generalizability with this standard. It is all too easy to use the vague indictment of low generalizability against studies that we may happen to question or disagree with.

## Is Generalizability Really That Important?

The discussion thus far has presupposed that generalizability between laboratory and life is, as some have implied, the ultimate question about research. We have to justify our laboratory studies by showing that they can be applied to the real world. But so far we have argued that we have no objective or quantifiable indexes of generalizability. Indeed we do not even know how much we can reasonably expect, except to say that we would like to have as much as we can get.

One way to reduce the dissonance generated by this predicament is to take the position that generalizability may not be so vital after all. If a laboratory analogue of a life situation is a highly artificial facsimile of the real phenomenon, and if the analogue examines the effect of only one or two of the multiple factors that ordinarily operate in that situation, why should one expect high generalizability? Furthermore, the observation period is quite brief, the subjects are either suspicious and/or aware of the purpose or hypotheses, and the experimenter is apt to be biased. Do we really think that high generalizability is likely?

If the answer is a clear, "of course not," then why have we been doing these laboratory experiments for so long? One rationale (Eagly, 1978; Kelman, 1968) is that the laboratory experiment is the best analytical method we have for testing hypotheses about factors that, according to theories, should have potent effects. The highly controlled situation may be a liability to generalizability, but it is indispensable to the determination of causal relationships that are predicted from our explanatory theories.

Thus, an experiment by Schachter (1977) was designed to test the hypothesis that heavy cigarette smokers, unlike light smokers, monitored and regulated the nicotine concentrations in their bodies. Using specially made cigarettes of higher and lower than normal nicotine levels, he found that addicted smokers adjusted the number of cigarettes smoked, depending on their concentration of nicotine, to achieve their customary nicotine levels. Inexperienced smokers did not differ in smoking of the two types of cigarettes. Inasmuch as these specially made cigarettes are not commercially available, one would not be able to ascertain generalizability to real life, but the findings offer support for the explanatory model proposed by Schachter for a real-life behavior.

Similarly, laboratory experiments on misattribution (Valins, 1966) provide fake feedback about autonomic responses to test the possibility that such cues can affect emotional reactions to stimuli associated with those cues. This is a highly artificial situation that is markedly different from any conceivable real-life counterpart. While one might hope that the results may be applicable to real-life situations, the primary function of this experiment is to provide a controlled test of the hypothesized influence of one factor and not to produce a simulation of the process as it normally occurs every day.

The quest for generalizability between laboratory and life has focused too narrowly on the extent to which there is correlation between results of *individual* experiments and their respective specific naturalistic counterparts. As we have already argued, the cards are heavily stacked against the possibility of high generalizability of results of *individual* experiments. Greater agreement between laboratory and life involves the synthesis of the outcomes of numerous interrelated experiments, which are in turn used to formulate and test explanatory models and theories of the real-life situation. Strictly speaking, this is not a matter of generalization but one involving broad understanding, explanation, and prediction.

Even though individual experiments taken one at a time may have low generalizability, when their outcomes are taken as a whole and used to develop and test more comprehensive conceptual models of the phenomenon, we may be better able to apply our knowledge to the real world. However, we should not equate application based on this level of understanding with generalizability of specific findings. Viewed from this different perspective, the concern with generalizability appears to have been misguided and misleading. In one sense this assessment is fortunate because, as noted earlier, the problems of measuring generalizability may be insurmountable.

Other, related issues may better justify our concern. Instead of concentrating on a strategy of first doing laboratory experiments and then checking out their results against naturalistic analogues, perhaps we need to expend greater effort toward more detailed and careful naturalistic descriptions of phenomena (Silverman, 1977; Tunnell, 1977). We need these types of descriptions if we hope to identify the most fruitful variables to use in our laboratory experiments. Lazarus and Launier (1978), for example, argue for this alternative emphasis in research on stress. Departing from the view implicit in earlier laboratory experiments (Lazarus, 1968), they feel it is premature to test hypotheses in the laboratory until a more detailed naturalistic description of stress phenomena is achieved.

After we obtain these more intensive studies of a descriptive variety about the phenomena as they occur under natural circumstances, we will have a more vivid and accurate picture. We will be better able to construct valid experimental analogues of the phenomena to use in the laboratory, to test our theories about underlying processes that determine behavior. Only then will we be able to truly increase the correspondence between the laboratory and life. As Hovland (1959) concluded after he found low generalizability for research on persuasive communication, it is important to realize that the role of the two types of studies is different. Hypothesis generation is best based on naturalistic studies, while hypothesis testing is the function of the laboratory experiments. Progress is best achieved by combining the two rather than pitting them against each other, since neither method is the one ultimate road to knowledge.

## References

Bandura, A. *Aggression: A Social Learning Analysis.* Englewood Cliffs, N.J.: Prentice-Hall, 1973.

Cartwright, D. "Risk Taking by Individuals and Groups: An Assessment of Research Employing Choice Dilemmas." *Journal of Personality and Social Psychology,* 1971, *20,* 361–378.

Cooley, C. H. *Human Nature and the Social Order.* New York: Scribner's, 1902.

Darley, J. M., and Latané, B. "Bystander Intervention in Emergencies: Diffusion of Responsibility." *Journal of Personality and Social Psychology,* 1968, *8,* 377–383.

Eagly, A. H. "Sex Differences in Influencibility." *Psychological Bulletin,* 1978, *85,* 86–116.

Hovland, C. I. "Reconciling Conflicting Results Derived from Experimental and Survey Studies on Attitude Change." *American Psychologist,* 1959, *14,* 8–17.

Kelman, H. C. *A Time to Speak: On Human Values and Social Research.* San Francisco: Jossey-Bass, 1968.

Kogan, H., and Wallach, M. A. *Risk Taking: A Study in Cognition and Personality.* New York: Holt, Rinehart and Winston, 1964.

Lazarus, R. S. "Emotions and Adaptation: Conceptual and Empirical Relations." In W. J. Arnold (Ed.), *Nebraska Symposium on Motivation.* Vol. 13. Lincoln: University of Nebraska Press, 1968.

Lazarus, R. S., and Launier, R. "Stress-Related Transactions Between Person and Environment." In L. A. Pervin and M. M. Lewis (Eds.), *Perspectives in Interactional Psychology*. New York: Plenum Press, 1978.

Mead, G. H. *Mind, Self, and Society*. Chicago: University of Chicago Press, 1934.

Orne, M. T. "Hypnosis, Motivation, and the Ecological Validity of the Psychological Experiment." In W. J. Arnold and M. M. Page (Eds.), *Nebraska Symposium on Motivation*. Vol. 18. Lincoln: University of Nebraska Press, 1970.

Piliavin, I. M., Rodin, J., and Piliavin, J. A. "Good Samaritanism: An Underground Phenomenon?" *Journal of Personality and Social Psychology*, 1969, *13*, 289-299.

Rosenthal, R. *Experimenter Effects in Behavior Research*. 2nd ed.) New York: Appleton-Century-Crofts, 1976.

Schachter, S. "Nicotine Regulation in Heavy and Light Smokers." *Journal of Experimental Psychology*, 1977, *106*, 5-12.

Shrauger, J. S., and Schoeneman, T. J. "Symbolic Interactionist View of Self-Concept: Through the Looking Glass Darkly." *Psychological Bulletin*, 1979, *86*, 549-573.

Silverman, I. "Why Social Psychology Fails." *Canadian Psychological Review*, 1977, *18*, 353-358.

Stein, A. H., Friedrich, L. K., and Vondracek, F. "Television Content and Young Children's Behavior." In J. P. Murray, E. A. Rubenstein, and G. A. Comstock (Eds.), *Television and Social Behavior*. Vol. 2: *Television and Social Learning*. Washington, D.C.: U.S. Government Printing Office, 1972.

Tunnell, G. B. "Three Dimensions of Naturalness: An Expanded Definition of Field Research." *Psychological Bulletin*, 1977, *84*, 426-437.

Valins, S. "Cognitive Effects of False Heart Rate Feedback." *Journal of Personality and Social Psychology*, 1966, *4*, 400-408.

Weber, S. J., and Cook, T. D. "Subject Effects in Laboratory Research: An Examination of Subject Roles, Demand Characteristics, and Valid Inferences." *Psychological Bulletin*, 1972, *77*, 273-295.

Willems, E. P., and Raush, H. L. (Eds.). *Naturalistic Viewpoints in Psychology*. New York: Holt, Rinehart and Winston, 1969.

*John Jung is professor of psychology, California State University, Long Beach.*

*Psychology's disenchantment with itself stems mainly*
*from a stilted view of the scientific enterprise.*

# Life and the Laboratory

## B. Richard Bugelski

In the last few years a growing disenchantment has been demonstrated by psychologists of various stripes or persuasions with the apparent, to them, lack of progress or emptiness of their chosen specialties. A particularly striking illustration of this malaise is Silverman's (1977) paper entitled "Why Social Psychology Fails." The title makes it obvious that for Silverman, at least, the efforts of social psychologists over the last century have proved unsatisfactory. Silverman cites a number of social psychologists who apparently share his views. Implicit and explicit in Silverman's paper is the notion that the methodology of social psychology is not equal to its mission. It is not leading to satisfactory answers to the questions some social psychologists believe to be important. One such question mentioned by Silverman addresses the impact of television violence on the behavior of young viewers. Governmental committees in the United States and Canada could get no incisive and definitive answers from social psychologists who had studied the problem. Perhaps the question Silverman should have addressed is: What is the mission of social psychology? Whatever this mission is, it may not be the development of a capacity to influence a parliamentary body subject to contradictory influences and interests.

The distress felt by Silverman for social psychology is echoed in other areas of the psychological arena. The field of clinical psychology has been smarting under the sting of criticism for several decades. At first, the early criticisms of Eysenck (1952) were ignored, down-graded, or rejected; but the persistent claim that 70 percent of psychotherapy patients recovered whether or not they were treated could not be silenced. Clinicians began to change their ways—they gave up projective tests, turned to one or another form of behavior therapy, or, finding a saving grace in the high ratio of possible patients to available clinicians, turned to community psychology without defining it or determining any methodology by which a community could be treated or immunized. One could reject personal psychotherapy not because it was ineffective but because there were not enough psychotherapists to handle the problem. A finer example of face-saving would be difficult to find. Clinical psychologists have not publicly recanted and turned to other trades; they still try to act as if they had a viable methodology and try to avoid contact with criticism. The recent book by Gross (1978), which amounts to a devastating, if polemical attack on psychotherapy, received only perfunctory attention in the leading journal of psychological book reviews, *Contemporary Psychology.*

The despair felt by social and clinical psychologists is not restricted to just those branches of psychology. Nowhere more than in the field of learning psychology has there been such soul-searching self-criticism. Several illustrations follow. In 1969 Gardner and Gardner reported an unusual study involving teaching an ape to use American sign language. The work caught the public fancy and other studies were quickly initiated with one or another variation of sign language being employed by the investigators. Over the years various complaints and criticisms were brought up but ignored by the investigators. It was not until recently that some investigators themselves (Terrace, 1979; Savage-Rumbaugh, Rumbaugh, and Boysen, 1980) raised the question seriously as to whether the apes were really using language or merely indulging in conditioned discriminatory behavior. According to Savage-Rumbaugh and others, ape language is not at all like human language beyond the most elementary signing operations of a human baby. Chimpanzees and other apes cannot talk about absent objects by way of conversation, description, or other information communication devices. They do not use the signs to represent objects or actions; all they do is indicate their desires. No ape would bother to say "the door is open," should such be the case. It would, of course, ask by one form of struggle or another (including signs) that a closed door be opened if it wanted to get out of a room and exits were closed. What Savage-Rumbaugh and her colleagues say, in effect, is that the apes are not using language in any human sense and that the methods of studying ape signing operations should be modified to apply to cognitive competencies that underlie symbolic processes. Note that they do not suggest that the projects might well be abandoned.

The last two decades have witnessed the wholesale adoption of the computer by learning psychologists. Instead of being used as a calculator, the computer has been proposed as a model of a human learner. The only problem with such models is that the computer does not learn. So? Let the computer do what it can do and ignore the learning problems that have puzzled generations of earlier psychologists. The computer was affectionately adopted by cognitive psychologists because it could encode and decode (apparently these are also human functions although no one ever noticed them before the appearance of the computer). The computer can also store and retrieve; it can search and process in parallel as well as in series. It can store some items for a short time, hence short-term memory. It can also store items forever (that should have given pause to some of the researchers). The fact that the computer's memory bank can be erased completely was another point rather blithely ignored. Human memories are not erased so quickly or completely except by death. Computers do not make mistakes, either, unless programmed to do so. Yet human error was no obstacle to memory modelers.

The short happy life of short-term memory can serve as an example of learning psychologists' frustrations. Starting with the findings of the Petersons (1959), psychologists spent a decade investigating and exploring short-term memory. The fact that short-term memory really meant that people could remember rather briefly only a little of some rapidly exposed, unfamiliar, nonsensical material that could not be rehearsed in a one-trial situation did not seem to impress the researchers. A proper question for the researchers to ask might have been: What does one remember from one brief encounter with unfamiliar material and how long can one remember the material if rehearsal is prevented? This would at least have led to an examination of the effects of a first learning trial. But the short-term memory researchers proceeded to build models with boxes and flow charts showing materials being ejected from short-term stores or transferred to long-term stores. The alleged ejection was explained on the grounds that apparently there had been no transfer. If there was transfer, there was no ejection. Never was there a happier situation: one could have it both ways. Why no one postulated an intermediate memory may be regarded as a strange omission. In any event, short-term memory has been put aside; it is not talked about so much today. The current fads are memory structures, themes, schemata, and organization.

Recently Estes (1980) took the computer to task. He pointed out that computers do not, in fact, act like humans; they do not take account of various attributes of an experience. They get no feel for the material. In storing a series of numbers mixed in with some letters, they do not have even vague ideas of where the numbers or letters were in the series although they can reproduce the list perfectly in a way no human could. They cannot answer the question: Were the letters in the middle? Scattered? Estes points out that humans are time oriented, computers are list oriented; computers retain information all-or-none, humans retain partial amounts; the human is dependent upon his past experience, the computer is not; the human makes use of context, the computer does not; and so on. Estes concludes that human memory does not, in a literal sense, store anything, but simply changes as a function of experience. Estes' statement will be ignored, of course, by all the psychologists with access to computer terminals.

Sometimes the disenchantment comes from outside the field. The invention of the intelligence test by Binet has been hailed as perhaps the greatest and the only readily applicable result of psychological studies. Today the intelligence test is under fire in various states, notably California, where it will be against the law to test children to determine IQ. The greatest single development in psychology is about to become illegal.

In the remainder of this chapter I shall explore some of the reasons for the disenchantment, malaise, disaffection, and disgruntlement facing many psychologists today and consider what, if anything, can be done about such disturbances.

## A Historical Perspective:
## Psychology and the Nature of Science

A brief look at the origins of modern psychology suggests that our current discontent is not unique to the discipline. Just prior to World War II, psychology was a rather small establishment. It held its annual meetings on university campuses, and the entire membership could be accommodated in one auditorium where members listened to discourses on topics no one ventures to discuss today. Psychology was an academic offshoot of philosophy departments. It had no particular justification or mission beyond the interests of its students. Some earlier empirically minded philosophers had chosen to take an experimental or laboratory approach to some philosophical problems—mind, will, intellect, sensory experience, and so forth. University administrations were not too concerned about the split in philosophy departments. Philosophy departments had always been around (they were the first academic disciplines), and their internal squabbles were of no great concern. They had never been subjected to the test of public utility or relevance. No one ever questioned the propriety of philosophy, and administrators rarely raised the question of the desirability of psychology departments. Had there been any serious question, it is unlikely that psychology departments would ever have been established.

One very important source of compounding of psychology's crisis of confidence stems from its drive toward professionalism. Shortly after World War II we saw an expansion in psychology or at least in the number of psychologists obtaining Ph.D. degrees and going off into the world of psychotherapy. The experiences in the war, the shortage of psychiatrists, the obstacles to a medical degree, and the rewarding prospects in clinical psychology proved enormously attractive. The Veterans Administration, desperate for help, subsidized psychology departments, as did the granting agencies of the federal government, and psychology became big business. Ph.D.s multiplied and went out to practice a science that had yet to show that it had applications. A great controversy arose about training, with clinicians urging a nonresearch degree while the academicians insisted on science first. The controversy is still alive, but some institutions now grant the PsyD, a doctorate of dubious distinction.

Professionalism involves an investment of money and time for preparation. Once the status of a professional is acquired, psychologists find it difficult to turn back or away from the training bought at such costs. The situation is similar in a bureaucracy. Once established, the bureaucracy cannot or does not dissolve itself. The famous March of Dimes established to cure polio prospered and grew; with its help polio was conquered. The March of Dimes kept marching; the professional management, now securely established, adopted another problem for itself and the personnel carried on. Now it collects money to prevent birth defects. It was a wise choice as there will probably always be some kinds of birth defects to combat. Similarly, psychologists licensed to engage in psychotherapy will engage in psychotherapy whether the activity proves useful or not. In either case, the demand for their services might well even expand. Even with new developments, those trained in older ways will continue the ancient practices until they retire. The situation is the same for trained academicians or scientists. They continue to ply their trades regardless of success or lack thereof.

At this point, it may be useful to consider psychology's discomfiture as it relates to the nature of science itself. Long ago James Conant (1953) described science as a kind of game wherein the scientist tried to find answers to questions that bothered him. The interesting point made by Conant was that any answer inevitably brought along with it more, perhaps many more, questions than it answered. New questions constantly arose; questions no one was smart enough to think of before the earlier questions had been answered. What is more, the questions always seemed more important than the just acquired answers, so that anything known became petty, old hat, unimportant, or at least relatively so. In short, according to Conant, scientists could never rest on their laurels or be satisfied even temporarily with what they discovered. The new problems outweighed the old in importance.

Kuhn makes a similar point. He argues that science itself is a matter of puzzle-solving and that only puzzle-solving people should aspire to being scientists. I find this description of science appealing because I always used to describe my course in the psychology of learning as analogous to the *New York Times* Sunday crossword puzzle. Solving the puzzle was a feat of no practical value. Sometimes one learned something that helped solve future crossword puzzles, but as far as anything practical or useful was concerned, that was about it. My course promised no help of any kind to anyone and would be of no appeal to anyone but the kind of person who enjoyed working on puzzles. This might seem like a rather poor reward for students, but I pointed to the philosophy department, which, as far as anyone knew, had not produced a single universally satisfying practical application about anything. I included all of the philosophy departments of all time in my remarks. Did I need to justify my course further? Need I have pointed out that it keeps psychology students and professors off the streets? But they are getting paid for it, said my students. But so is everyone else getting paid; some on welfare, obviously for doing nothing; others in various offices, stores, or factories, presumably for doing something. Yet the practical utility of what millions of people do for a living is easily questioned. Do we need a sports commentator on every television station, for example? Do we need professional athletic teams in every conceivable sport in every city foolish enough to spend taxpayers' money on a stadium? Are athletic entertainers more important than psychology professors? In short, I told my students, psychology, so far as it aims to be a science, is a matter of puzzle-solving that somehow has gained public support.

Now the fact that psychology (in so far as it is a science and not a professional art) is a puzzle-solving enterprise means that from time to time it will encounter puzzles that cannot be solved by present traditions, methods, and skills, in short, by the disciplinary matrix. Such failures will result in a variety of reactions; some scientists will despair and look over neighbors' fences at the greener grass; others will persist, doggedly trying to solve the new puzzles with old methods; still others will look for new methods, question old assumptions, even develop new skills.

The basic reason for the current malaise, then, to put it bluntly, is that psychologists have not been bright enough to ask satisfying questions, or to do research of such quality that they would be pleased to find answers to the questions they do ask. Such an indictment cannot be taken personally by anyone; anyone who does take it personally can rationalize that the problems psychologists face are extremely complex and many-sided with countless variables that are difficult to control. If such a rationalization helps, anyone is entitled to nourish it. It is still a fact that, in the face of the nature of our problems, we are unable to come up with fast, easy solutions and acceptable applications.

Silverman (1977) complains about the training of social psychologists, which leads to the failure of students to formulate and solve problems in real-life settings. But the only training that can be given to graduate students consists of the skills, traditions, and problem-solving techniques possessed by the present staff. How can they teach better than they do? There is nothing wrong with this situation. It is exactly what goes on in all academic departments from astronomy to zoology. It is the character of scientific training to pattern students after the ways and methods of the faculty, so that they work on problems that interest the faculty, not on problems that students might find in the real world. The traditions and interests of the faculty comprise what Kuhn (1977) now calls the "disciplinary matrix"—he used to call it the "paradigm" until he found the latter word meant too many things to too many people. So long as a particular disciplinary matrix appears to work, no great number of people will be disturbed. It is only when the disciplinary matrix does not seem to be making progress, and when some other matrix appears to work better or is apparently encroaching on one's territory, that dissatisfaction develops. For such points, Kuhn speaks of scientific revolutions. What must be recognized from Kuhn's writings is that, as mentioned before, the intelligence of trainers of graduate students is only as good as it is. They cannot train students to be wiser than themselves; they are not wise enough to do so.

The present discomfiture may represent the first signs of a revolution in social psychology, a revolution that may or may not prove to be an advance. If social psychology turns to the world of real-life events, it may find itself ill-equipped to solve the problems that are crushingly obvious: war, poverty, inflation, industrial strife, racism, overpopulation, lack of productivity, unemployment, and the decline of natural resources, among others.

## A Positive Outlook

The causes of the current discontent have been suggested above. It is time to turn to solutions, or at least, to a more positive view. The solutions will not be easy to accept by those who have been participating in the wrong game.

**The Question of Application.** Science is not concerned with applications. Two great and commonly acknowledged advances are the Copernican revolution and the Darwinian theory of evolution. In neither case are there any immediate practical applications. The *Naval Almanac,* the workbook of navigators, takes no account of the fact that the earth circles the sun. As far as the *Naval Almanac* is concerned, the sun rises in the east and sets in the west and certain stars are at certain points in the sky at particular moments in time. Navigators can determine their positions on the ocean or in the sky by pretending that the heavenly bodies orbit the earth. The findings of astronomers have enabled scientists to deduce the existence of and to discover previously unknown planets, but no travel agent is yet booking trips to Uranus.

As for Darwin's monumental discovery, people view chimpanzees in the zoo and the chimpanzees view the people. In the vast majority of cases, it does not occur to either species to consider actual kinship. Hereditary laws do enable cattle breeders to improve their stock, but that was more Mendel's contribution than Darwin's. At the human level, applied genetics is more of a moral problem than a practical issue—we can hope that it remains so. The problem of what kind or kinds of people we might want in the future is truly a mind boggler.

**Progress.** There is another problem: applications are commonly related to progress, a difficult concept at best. Philosophers do not know what progress is, much less whether or not it is desirable. The invention of television is progress of a sort, in one direction; yet had it never been invented, the problem of illiteracy among our young might not have surfaced. However, without television we would not see our astronauts landing on the moon, a scientific or at least engineering event whose practical application may never materialize except for the development of the instrumentation that got them there. The exploration of Saturn will answer a lot of astronomers' questions, but the world at large may profit but little except in the satisfaction of curiosity among the curious. Splitting the atom resulted in the hydrogen bomb, which brought its own problems. Atomic energy has its advocates and detractors. The eventual application of some scientific discovery does not carry any guarantees of positive value; curing cancer will increase the problems of caring for a larger aging population. One might well be a bit concerned about progress.

**The Slow March of Science.** Let us return to the failure of social psychology or any other psychological specialty. There has been no failure unless one has some personal criterion for success. Science, whether in the form of social psychology or any other variety, plods on. It does what it can, what it has to do. Scientists are no more free than anyone else to do other than what they do. They are bound by their backgrounds, training, and heredity (if solving puzzles is a hereditary trait) to attack certain problems in certain ways (the only ways they know). When the methods are inadequate to the problem, they usually give up, the problem is set aside and forgotten, perhaps for generations. It took thousands of years for some ideas to surface. The invention of the zero took centuries after a sort of useful arithmetic had been devised by the Babylonians. In short, what is the hurry? In this context, Pratt (1937) wisely argued that psychology should remain in the library and the laboratory for a long time to come. How long is a long time? Spence (1951) suggested that in about five hundred years psychology might amount to something. Certainly no one except the extreme optimist should look forward to progress in one lifetime. What progress one might observe is probably only movement, and possibly movement in the wrong direction.

**Science: A Self-Correcting Pursuit.** A second point, more palliative than solution, is that science is self-correcting. The Ptolemaic theory did give way to the Copernican view although that took a few centuries. Newton had to bow to Einstein after only three hundred years. Scientific discoveries of a smaller order take less time. In his *Structure of Science,* Nagle (1979) illustrates the weakness of social science by describing a study in which married women employed in a factory were found to be absent more often than single women. Nagle cautions against the hasty judgment that it would benefit the employer to hire single women because a subsequent study revealed the fact that when single women performed the same amount of housework as did the married women, the absentee rate was the same. The true cause of absenteeism was thus housework and not marriage. Describing the first study, Nagle was trying to point out the shoddiness of social science; he was concerned about jumping at conclusions. But there was the second study. What he actually was pointing out was that science was self-correcting. The truth did come out. Ignoring Nagle, the employer would still be wise and logical in employing only single women since they, as a group, did less housework and since it is far easier to discover marital status than amount of time spent doing household chores.

What is more serious is to discover that an earlier model or conclusion was completely fallacious or unwarranted; this, too, happens frequently. Lachman, Lachman, and Butterfield (1979) describe a number of memory models that succeeded each other by a process of successive corrections of earlier defects. By the time the final corrections had been made, the original model was completely discredited, and no viable alternate had emerged from the mountains of research involved. The pessimistic psychologist could well shrug off the whole effort as a colossal waste of time. But isn't all puzzle-solving? What appears to be challenging and positive today has a way of becoming old hat and even wrong tomorrow. Today's truths have a way of becoming tomorrow's misguided opinions of the past.

By far the greatest or most serious problem is the lack of sophistication in theoretical thinking. Theories are not evaluated intellectually prior to being subjected to research aimed at confirmation. One psychologist very seriously concerned about theories was Hull (1943). He pondered the philosophy of science and consulted physicists, philosophers, psychoanalysts, physiologists, and mathematicians, about the nature of basic approaches and assumptions, and about what could be taken for granted and what had to be evaluated. Although his own theoretical program did not survive the headlong plunge into computer models, he did think about what he was doing. He was concerned about axioms, definitions, and postulates; he particularly emphasized an operational approach. The need for sound operational definitions of their constructs appears to have no great interest for modern researchers—their only concern appears to be one of developing operations that can be performed by a computer. There is nothing wrong with what the computer produces in its outputs; the question is with the inputs. We can best appreciate the problem by turning to a currently active area in research, the image.

Some will recall that the image was once regarded as the great tool of thinking and learning-by-association by philosophers and early structural psychologists. They never defined the image operationally, but too, what seemed at the time the reasonable view that images were reproductions of previous sensory experiences. Such a definition has no experimental value. It is not something anyone can manipulate in a laboratory. Watson (1914) rejected such a construct, calling it the ghost of sensation. About four decades later Leuba (1940) suggested that images were conditioned sensations. Had he not used the term sensation he might have arrived at a more operational definition. In the 1960s and 1970s the image enjoyed a research revival, but again no real effort was made toward operationalizing the term. Images became some kind of representations. While most workers in the field decried the notion of pictures in the mind, the term *representation* was certainly no better; at best it was a euphemism at a somewhat greater distance from whatever reality an image might possess. Working with representations, psychologists turned to even more esoteric euphemisms, such as *schema, theme, structure,* and so forth to account for alleged internal, mental experiences or processes. Whatever progress had been made in psychology in the last century was curtailed by this revival of mentalism.

True, some workers, such as Paivio (1971), defined imagery (not the image) in an operational way by using words for imagery that had been rated by college students. A particular word could be said to be of high or low imagery value and assigned a numerical rating. That at least appeared operational. The problem here was that the operations the students went through to determine the ratings were never operationalized beyond the instruction to students to give a high rating if an image occurred quickly and a low one if it occurred slowly or not at all. The image itself was never described operationally. With such a tool at his disposal, however, Paivio was able to produce a large number of interesting findings about how associations are retained and about the relationship of language to meaning. But Paivio's work did not represent a breakthrough. Other psychologists did not hail it as a great development in psychology — they went on instead studying representations which they transformed into propositions. They then fed verbal or symbolic formulations of propositions into their computers. Their successes so far seem to some to be infinitesimal and certainly irrelevant to how the mind works, allegedly the concern of cognitive psychologists. A great deal of further work will undoubtedly emerge and be published, but it is doubtful that we will discover how the mind works until someone develops appropriate operational definitions for it.

The failure to examine basic assumptions and develop operational definitions should be not only clear but also rankling to any psychologist who has taught elementary psychology. When discussing vision, for example, the introductory course instructor draws a picture of the eye on the blackboard and traces various energies through the cornea, lens, retina, optic chiasm, and area 17, leading the students on in the notion that they are learning about vision. When the instructor finishes with area 17, he or she goes on to discuss audition. At no point in the presentation has "seeing" been discussed. Nor will "hearing" be discussed after he or she is through with the cochlea, basilar membrane, and the temporal lobes. The simple fact is that psychologists do not

know what "seeing" is, and they mask their ignorance by presenting some elementary physics and physiology. They would do better to face up to the question of what seeing and hearing are and investigate the problems that can be
operationally stated.

To return to imagery, we find that similar escape hatches are employed.
Skinner (1974), for example, defines imagery as inner seeing. As we do not
know what outer seeing is, this definition is not of much help. As a suggestion
of what might be more profitable, I have suggested (Bugelski, 1977) that an
image is a conditioned response — not a conditioned sensation as Leuba presented it. We have images when we react (internally) to a conditioned stimulus
in somewhat the same way that we did to the unconditioned stimulus. To illustrate: when we look at an apple, something happens to us — we call it *seeing*.
Later, if the word apple has accompanied the visual presentation, we can have
some approximation of the original reaction to the previously seen apple from
merely hearing the word. Such a response may or may not be of much importance. In various experimental settings, however, as in the case of mnemonic
learning, it may have a powerful effect. Because images are unobservable,
experimenters must work with them as other scientists do with their hypotheti-
cal constructs, such as black holes, interferon, genes, and the growing number
of kinds of subatomic particles, with the postulated variables necessarily oper-
ating at least one stage removed from direct observation.

Another illustration may be derived from memory studies. In the good
old days of functionalism, it was the accepted position by psychologists that
there was no such thing as memory, that is, no such faculty or mechanism,
machine, structure or any other kind of box, storage compartment, or whatever. People remembered or forgot, and the business of psychologists was to
discover why they did either and both. A great many interesting puzzles were
solved and they resulted, as might have been expected, in more interesting
puzzles. Sometime in the late 1950s, psychologists forgot the old wisdom and
restored memory as some kind of storage place, suitably described by boxes
with arrows, populated by various activities — serial memory, parallel memory, total searches, and retrieval operations.

We have already noted the conclusion of Estes (1980) that memory
changes with experience. This is not quite good enough. What Estes should
have said is that what we call memory is not something that in itself exists and
changes. We still either remember or forget, and the reason for it is that we
change; that is, something takes place in our nervous systems when we learn
something so that we are now different from what we were before and conse-
quently can and will behave differently. Sometimes the change that we demonstrate by learning itself changes so that we can no longer behave in the new
way. If I fail to recall a name that I learned, it is not because something is
wrong with my memory but because something has changed in me; I am no

longer the same person, the one who could remember the name. The change might be temporary or permanent. In any case, there has been a change. Any theoretical speculations that postulate some kind of storage compartments in some even more hazily described mind are doomed to failure and will lead to disillusionment by those who placed their faith in such theories.

Another aspect of memory research might illustrate the point. Researchers record reports of their subjects as if these reports represented what a subject recalls or remembers. They ignore the now well-established fact that subjects are biased in their responses, but in this instance the bias is to appear intelligent, orderly, and organized. What they recall is one thing, what they report is another. Just for interest consider listening to a news broadcast (without any instruction to remember) and let someone later on ask: What was on the news? You will find that there will be no order or organization to your recall but your report will be, if not "nothing of any consequence," an effort to tell what you think your listener might wish to know. You will discard or disregard items you do recall; you will not relate the items in the sequence in which they appeared, but perhaps in some relation to importance or the like. If you try to recall a novel or television show, the items you recall will not be orderly, in sequence, or organized. Events from the middle might occur to you before events from the start. Trivia you would not mention might impose themselves. Your actual report would be in great variance with the nature of your recall. Researchers in memory have learned a lot about reports and very little about memory.

As the puzzle-solving operations of psychological investigators go on, researchers discover new ways of viewing problems, puzzles, or questions. In that sense, science is self-corrective. Sometimes it takes a long time to arrive at a new insight, a new intuition, a new set. A crossword puzzle that looks impossible one day might be solved the next because a new set is adopted with respect to some word. The solver has not become smarter or brighter in the intervening period. It took some sixty years of work in the area of conditioning before Mowrer (1960) came to look at Pavlovian conditioning as a matter of emotional reactions rather than simple glandular or motor association to some stimulus. Pavlov had selected the salivary reflex for his own good reasons. According to Mowrer, he was not only wrong in doing so, but very, very wrong. He should have known better, but as I have tried to show repeatedly in this chapter, no one can know better than he does at any given time; someday he or she might, perhaps for the most trivial and fortuitous reasons.

The illustrations presented above should suggest that science is not an enterprise that supplies answers upon demand. It is not an instant satisfier. Some questions are complex and difficult with many potential answers to be considered, tested, and explored. For a recent *New York Times* article (Mermelstein, 1979), an investigator queried twenty outstanding economists about the cure for inflation. He got, in effect, twenty different answers. Only three economists agreed on a particular suggestion, which was denounced by the others. Now, we know that economics is a "dismal science." This does not lead economists to abandon their chosen fields. They blithely study inflation while suffering from it. There may be an answer to inflation, but those in positions to take action are too impatient or unable to try one of the twenty remedies at a time and wait for long-term effects. They could try all twenty at once, and if inflation continued we could then judge that none of the suggestions was any good. But even here we could be wrong because some of the suggestions are mutually contradictory to begin with, and the effects could cancel out.

The answer to the failures and weaknesses of psychology is not to abandon the laboratory and turn to more naturalistic and field observations, as Silverman has suggested. If we do that we will see cannon balls falling faster than feathers and will never find out about gravity, vacuums, outer space, and weightlessness; we will begin to see aggression as a natural human trait that must inevitably lead to war; we will see territoriality in subway rush hours even if there is no room between bodies. What we should recognize, of course, is that the laboratory is not a building or a room with fixed walls and do-not-disturb signs. The laboratory is a method, the method of experimentation based on the reasonably correct descriptions provided by John Stuart Mill. In research we conduct controlled experiments. We vary one thing at a time, and we measure the independent and dependent variables as best we can. Those are the rules of the game. In the case of some problems we may not be clever enough to arrange the controls effectively as of now. In that case we may have to postpone investigation of some problems and turn to those that are amenable to study. As long as the public supports science, science will continue solving puzzles. Sometimes the solutions will have some practical applications.

The public support of science itself needs some mention. The support is not active but quite indirect, a matter of assignment of some tax receipts to universities and institutes. Generally the public is quite unaware of what goes on and how the money is spent. The public has no say in the matter, and politicians dispense funds, sometimes grudgingly, for reasons that often are remote from scientific interests. Military or chauvinistic motives may underlie space exploration. Industrial profits may dictate other scientific explorations. There is a general curiosity factor in the public as well as among politicians that may play a role—the long history of scientific development has resulted in some applications that are regarded highly. Science is part of education, and education has achieved the status of an undeniable value. It is fortunate for scientists that science has become respectable. There are, to be sure, occasional anti-intellectual periods and people but, in general, almost any kind of project that can be called scientific will get some support. The study of volcanoes is underwritten by people who are quite safe from eruptions and who do not expect the scientists to stop the volcanic explosions or do much more than, perhaps, predict the time of some future blast. A successful prediction of a volcano eruption on some uninhabited island would be received with general satisfaction.

It is easy to criticize the efforts of laboratory investigators, especially in the social sciences. Senator Proxmire has earned the adulation of a smirking public by his, perhaps, earnest efforts. If the senator, however, recognized that scientific work is at least as complex and difficult as conducting the government, he might well ask himself what he has accomplished, or, for that matter, what the rest of the Senate has done to improve the lot of mankind since he has been in office. Social psychologists, like scientists in other areas, are doing the best they can. Their failures, if they can be called such, frequently result from too hasty an effort to find applications. In such hurried or outer-guided research they might not ask the right questions. Too often they have tried to prove something to support their personal views on social issues. Such personal involvement gets in the way of the clear formulation of problems or questions. There is nothing wrong with social psychology except for the urge to be effective. It is not the purpose of science to be effective. It needs only to answer questions of how variables act and interact, a process that benefits greatly from hindsight.

## References

Bugelski, B. R. "Imagery and Verbal Behavior." *Journal of Mental Imagery*, 1977, *1*, 39–52.

Conant, J. B. *Modern Science and Modern Man*. New York: Anchor Books, 1953.

Estes, W. K. "Is Human Memory Obsolete?" *American Scientist*, 1980, *68*, 62–69.

Eysenck, A. J. "The Effects of Psychotherapy." *Journal of Consulting Psychology*, 1952, *16*, 319–324.

Gardner, B. T., and Gardner, R. A. "Teaching Sign Language to a Chimpanzee." *Science*, 1969, *165*, 664–672.

Gross, M. L. *The Psychological Society*. New York: Random House, 1978.

Hull, C. L. *The Principles of Behavior*. New York: Appleton-Century-Crofts, 1943.

Kuhn, T. *The Essential Tension*. Chicago: University of Chicago Press, 1977.

Lachman, R., Lachman, J., and Butterfield, E. C. *Cognitive Psychology and Information Processing*. Hillsdale, N.J.: Erlbaum, 1979.

Leuba, C. "Images as Conditioned Responses." *Journal of Experimental Psychology*, 1940, *26*, 345–351.

Mermelstein, D. "The Threatening Economy." *New York Times*, Dec. 10, 1979.

Mowrer, O. H. *Learning Theory and Behavior*. New York: Wiley, 1960.

Nagle, E. *The Structure of Sciene*. Indianapolis, Ind.: Hackett Publishing, 1979.

Paivio, A. *Imagery and Verbal Processes*. New York: Holt, Rinehart and Winston, 1971.

Peterson, L. R., and Peterson, M. J. "Short-Term Retention of Individual Verbal Items." *Journal of Experimental Psychology*, 1959, *58*, 193–208.

Pratt, C. C. *The Logic of Modern Psychology*. New York: Macmillan, 1937.

Savage-Rumbaugh, E. S., Rumbaugh, D. M., and Boysen, M. "Do Apes Use Language?" *American Scientist*, 1980, *68*, 49–61.

Silverman, I. "Why Social Psychology Fails." *Canadian Psychological Review*, 1977, *18*, 353–358.

Skinner, B. F. *About Behaviorism.* New York: Knopf, 1974.

Spence, K. W. "Theoretical Interpretations of Learning." In S. S. Stevens (Ed.), *Handbook of Experimental Psychology.* New York: Wiley, 1951.

Terrace, H. S. "Is Problem-Solving Language?" *Journal of Experimental Analysis of Behavior,* 1979, *31,* 161–175.

Watson, J. *Behavior.* New York: Holt, Rinehart and Winston, 1914.

*B. Richard Bugelski is Distinguished Research Professor Emeritus,
State University of New York, Buffalo.*

*Positive social application of social science data requires*
*recognition of the power context within which*
*the social sciences exist.*

# On the Application of
# the Social Sciences

## David Bakan

There is a certain hope, especially in the academic, liberal, intellectual, social science community, that the human condition could be greatly improved if the yield of the social sciences could be brought to bear on the great contemporary social, political, and economic problems. One beholds the great discrepancy between the changes wrought by the application of the physical sciences — some of them very distinguished, and many of them at least powerful — and the relatively little of consequence from the academic social sciences.

The application of the physical sciences have brought us technological advances that no one can deny. Yet, there are also the great dangers from these technological advances: exhaustion of natural resources; pollution; poisoning; major upsets in the ecological balance of the world; and the worst of all threats, war, which has been made most technologically excellent — indeed technologically exquisite — by these same advances. The case is urged that by bringing the social sciences to bear on these problems, the benefits of the physical sciences may be more fully realized and the current high social costs of technology can be brought to a minimum. There appears to be a clear imperative to bring the social sciences to bear on the world, to match, and to compensate for the negative features of the application of the physical sciences.

I must confess that I long participated in this view I have outlined. It will be recalled that in 1954 the Supreme Court, in its landmark decision of *Brown* v. *Board of Education* of Topeka, Kansas, declared that separate educational facilities were inherently unequal and therefore unconstitutional. In the course of the court's deliberations, the researches of Professor Otto Klineberg of Columbia University on race differences were considered and cited. This, and some similar events, seemed to suggest that the social sciences might come to play a major role in connection with positive social change in the society. I am, however, quite pessimistic about such a possibility; although, I must quickly add, I also have a bit of guarded optimism. The considerations that I want to present bear on both my pessimism and my optimism. My pessimism arises from the recognition of the power context within which the social sciences function. My optimism arises from the bit of confidence I have that the very recognition of its place in that power context might itself be a factor in changing its place in that power context.

## Knowledge and Power

To suggest that the social sciences exist within a power context is, however, only to recognize that the social sciences are the same as any other enterprise, individual or collective, within society. Some years ago I was brought to review some of the factors associated with mental health. In the course of that study it became very apparent to me that there were basically two ways to look at psychological disturbance. One was to see it as an essentially individual phenomenon. Looking at it in this way, one considered the history of the individual, the native talents and defects, the individual's experiences, the individual's biology, and the individual's adjustment pattern. The other way, which I came to regard with considerably greater favor, was to view psychological disturbance as a social disturbance that only manifested itself in the individual. When I tried to summarize the way this social disturbance affected individuals, I identified three sets of factors: neglect, oppression, and diminution. Neglect is neglect of such necessary things as protection, education, and maintenance—including the necessary protective, educational, and maintaining milieu we call love. Oppression is the denial of basic freedoms, including denial of security of person, the ultimate form of oppression. Diminution is the kind of denial of one's validity as a person exemplified by the varieties of discrimination.

If we take this view of mental health, we can see at least two ways in which the power context is relevant. First, the power context is directly relevant in determining whether persons suffer from psychological disturbance; and who the victims will be, if any. Second, the power context bears on the fashioning of a social science enterprise that would, by regarding the whole problem of mental health from an exclusively individual-centered point of view, blind us to the power context of mental health in the first place.

I speak, almost in the same breath, of a subject—mental health—dealt with by the social sciences as associated with the power context, and of the social sciences themselves as being in the power context. This complexity, this reflexivity, arises from the very special connection that exists between knowledge and power.

What is the connection between knowledge and power? Francis Bacon said that knowledge is power. That sentence may well be regarded as a major motto of world experience since at least the sixteenth century. What it asserts is too obvious to need defense. Technology is a main example. The victory of the Battle of Midway during World War II was a direct result of the fact that American cryptologists had deciphered the Japanese code and were reading all their radio messages. What is more interesting and less obvious are those efforts by some people to maintain power by maintaining ignorance in others. Thus, for example, alluding once again to the history of blacks in the United States: After the relatively effective slave revolt led by Nat Turner in 1831 in Virginia was crushed, a wave of legislation to prohibit the education of slaves was passed. Similarly, the critical issue, to this very day, associated with the question of blacks in the United States centers around the question of educational opportunity. Indeed, Francis Bacon may only have been cribbing from the author of the Biblical words, "Know the truth, and the truth shall make you free."

It is hardly necessary to attempt a modern, empirical study to test Francis Bacon's or the Bible's hypothesis. Yet it is instructive at least to imagine a kind of chi-square study where the data are arranged in the by-now classical two-way table. Imagine such a table. Across the top, we have the two columns labeled "those who suffer" and "those who thrive." Now along the side, marking the rows, we have "those who know" and "those who don't know." We now count how many people there are in each cell. I am quite sure, without collecting any data, that the numbers of those who don't know and suffer, and of those who know and thrive, are considerably larger than the numbers in the remaining two groups.

The relationship between knowledge and power may be viewed from another perspective. The usual understanding of the relationship between knowledge and power as it is expressed in the Baconian maxim conceives of knowledge as a resource, a tool, or a means by which a person may increase the effectiveness of a plan. Indeed, it is interesting to see how the Baconian maxim became incorporated into our thinking. It came to be interpreted as the understanding of causation. Thus, to understand causation is to allow one to manipulate causes in order to achieve desired effects. And cause itself, through David Hume, John Stuart Mill, and modern positivistic and empiricist thought, came to be narrowly understood. That understanding is that causality is essentially co-occurrence of cause and effect; or better, observed co-occurrence *interpreted* as cause and effect.

However valuable that way of understanding causality may have been in the physical sciences, it is unfortunately far too narrow for understanding power as a social science phenomenon. For power, at least if it is to be appreciated properly, has to be understood as much broader than the application of narrow cause-effect linkages. Power must be understood as the way in which one person's mind can influence the mind of another. It is human mind and its power to influence plus the human mind and its susceptibility to influence by other minds that constitute the elements of power. The enumeration of the features of mind associated with power must be incomplete. But we can include the complexities of identity, thought and language, fears, shames, guilts, inferiority feelings, vanity, lust, anger, resentment, obligation, ambition, envy, vengefulness, loyalty, intimidation, conspiracy, deceit, collusion, craftiness, stubbornness, honesty, pride, passion, petulance, pettiness, nobility, sensitivity to justice, and the like. Causality, as understood by Hume and mimicked by so many in the modern world who would consider themselves scientific, is simply much too narrow. To insist on the doctrines of Hume as a norm for thought is to guarantee the impotence of whoever truly subscribes to that norm.

Indeed, I would enlarge the case that I am making. There are ideological features associated with the social sciences that seem contrived precisely because they are inappropriate to the exercise of power. I will not argue that such contrivance has been deliberate, although one should not shy away from that possibility. Even in the case of the physical sciences, there has been a fear on the part of the persons in political power that the growth of understanding of the nature of the physical world would take power away from them. Consider the Royal Society of London, the society in which Newton played such a prominent part and which was so critically responsible for the development of science in the Western world. When it was founded and granted a charter by the king, the members were required to agree that they would not take part in matters which were outside the terms of reference, and especially that they would take no part in the ongoing political and religious struggles. Now, those political and religious struggles were the critical power struggles of the day. Thus the granting of a license to the scientists of the day, and of support, was precisely on the condition that they remove themselves from the theaters of power struggles. As Arendt has suggested, one may well be tempted to see in this the birth of the modern scientific ideal of "objectivity" (1958, p. 271).

## David Hume and Joshua

Allow me to try to make this point about ideology and impotence a bit clearer by looking more closely at Hume's notion of causality and the general popularity of this notion among those social scientists who pride themselves on their objectivity, or their empiricism, or behavioralism, or positivism, or whatever other rubric is used to represent a commitment to the view of causality so well expressed by David Hume. Consider how dangerous or inappropriate Hume's notion would be in connection with something that critically involves power, such as warfare. According to David Hume one never can observe a causal relationship. Regarding things as causally connected is only the result of some frequent and uniform co-occurrence of events. Because of this, then, the idea of one event brings up the idea of the other event. Thus a habit of mind is formed. And like other habits, it is experienced as compulsion. And similarly, the seeming compulsory character of causality is merely a kind of projection of this habit of mind onto nature.

This view appears to be quite harmless and remote from power. However, if we allow only that there may be relationships between deceit and power, the significance of Hume for the powerlessness of the social sciences begins to become evident. Consider the story of the Battle of Ai, fought by Joshua, and reported in the Bible. I refer to the eighth chapter of the Book of Joshua. Joshua is interested in taking the city of Ai. He sends a party of warriors to hide close by the city. Joshua then leads the main body of his army toward the city. The king of Ai, seeing the army approach, comes out to fight Joshua. And then, as the text tells us,

> Joshua and all Israel made as if they were beaten before them, and fled by the way of the wilderness. And all the people that were in Ai were called together to pursue them: and they pursued after Joshua, and were drawn away from the city. And there was not a man left in Ai or Beth el, that went not out after Israel: and they left the city open, and pursued after Israel. And the Lord said unto Joshua, Stretch out the spear that is in thy hand toward Ai; for I will give it into thine hand. And Joshua stretched out his hand: and they entered into the city, and took it, and hasted and set the city on fire. And when the men of Ai looked behind them, they saw, and, beheld the smoke of the city ascended up to heaven, and they had no power to flee this way or that way; and the people that fled to the wilderness turned back upon the pursuers. And when Joshua and all Israel saw that the ambush had taken the city, and that the smoke of the city ascended, then they turned again and slew the men of Ai.

The essence of Joshua's strategy was that the people of Ai would think in the way David Hume described. The two ideas associated in the minds of the people of Ai were defeat and retreat; that is, since the Israelites were in retreat, it had to be that the cause of the retreat was defeat. Indeed, I am certain that they had a substantial body of experience of that particular co-occurrence.

Every ruse, every deception, characteristically works because the victim extrapolates a mere association into the future. If David Hume had offered his observation about association as a basis for teaching the reader how to deceive others, his observation would have some validity, however questionable its morality. But David Hume's descriptions of association have been taken as prescriptive for the scientific method, not as descriptive of stupidity or as descriptive of the state of mind of a likely loser in a power conflict in which a likely victor employs deceit.

But let us dwell on this a bit longer. Appreciating the role of Hume's notion of causality and co-occurrence as prescriptive may help us to understand the power position of contemporary social science. I have suggested thus far that Hume's observations as a model of the scientific method — as a model of how the scientist should think — is a critical factor in social science's impotence. I have suggested that associational thinking is the essential feature of the thinking of the victim of a ruse and that it is the basis for victimization. I have distinguished between just noting the existence of Hume's associational thinking among human beings, on the one hand, and the use of Hume's formula as an imperative and a model of scientific thought, on the other. As a matter of fact, it cannot be denied that people frequently engage in a kind of thinking in which they project past co-occurrences into the future. There is no question that such association is often factually justified.

While that is true, it can also be argued that the likelihood of achieving power in the world may depend on *transcending* in oneself the habit of mind described by Hume while taking advantage of such a habit of mind in others. Human dominion over nature and over other animals is quite precisely the consequence of humans' ability to transcend such mere associationism. Let us go back to Joshua for a moment. Clearly the people of Ai engaged in the kind of thinking to which Hume referred. They had learned the correlation of defeat with retreat. Having seen the co-occurrence of defeat with retreat, they had made the inference that defeat was the cause of retreat. Thus, when they saw the Israelites in retreat, they inferred that the cause of such an effect was a reality, that the Israelites had been defeated. Joshua, however, although not mistaking co-occurrence for causality, took full advantage of such associational thinking among the people of Ai.

Thus, the distinction that I am drawing is between observing a correlation between A and B and inferring a causal relationship between them, on the one hand — as the people of Ai did — and on the other knowing and making use of the existence of an association in others — as Joshua did. The point is almost banal: correlation means neither causality nor necessity. But stupid people take correlation for causality or necessity. Those who can transcend correlation in this way in themselves, but who are appropriately aware of it in others, can truly come to the point of acquiring the power — but over others — indicated in the Baconian maxim. In a situation of conflict, as in a war, each party gains advantage by knowing the opponents' associations and by transcending his own.

What bearing does this have on the problem of the social sciences and on the possible role of the social sciences in solving some of the problems that confront humankind at the present time? The huge influence of Hume as prescriptive in the social sciences tends to dictate a particular pattern of approach. The function of the social scientist is to identify the associations that characterize human behavior and human experience. The knowledge of these associations is then made available to those who determine policy, those who might then apply the knowledge through some strategem. Thus Professor Klineberg's research demonstrated that schools separated by race were associated with education of different quality; separate black schools were associated with inferior black education. Thus, the enlightened Supreme Court ordered the desegregation of the schools in order to equalize the quality of education for the races. The strategy is, however, based on the questionable assumption that the applier of the knowledge is wise and just; that while the project is clearly manipulative, it is manipulative in a way that leads to beneficial outcomes with justly distributed costs.

This mode of thinking is familiar enough. It certainly entails an appreciation of both modes of thought, the associative habit of mind of the king of Ai and its exploitation by Joshua. But in the development of our notions of science we have virtually converted Hume's paradigm into a prescription for how the scientist should think. Scientists have been urged, at least in their scientific roles, not to enter into the kind of thinking engaged in by Joshua. This has left a vacuum to be stepped into by power-oriented people, given to the use of strategem and unhampered by the common Humean socialization of the social scientist.

## Historical Perspective on the Social Sciences

There is some value in looking at some aspects of the development of the social sciences. The social sciences have been developing as self-conscious disciplines for about one hundred years. Before that time, the topics that we would now identify under the rubric of social science had a characteristically open connection with power. We can mention Aristotle, Plato, Machiavelli, Hobbes, Locke, Bentham, Adam Smith, John Stuart Mill, Karl Marx, and even Freud. Modern social science, however, tends to draw away from similarly addressing questions of power. Needless to say this applies less to contemporary Marxians and Freudians. But then, there are many who would not consider the Marxians and the Freudians to be social *scientists*. For part of the understanding of the word *scientist* has come to connote, precisely, one who withdraws from concern with matters of power.

Yet there is a certain amount of irony here. At least since 1913, when John B. Watson, the founder of behaviorism, announced that "prediction and control" were the goals of a scientific psychology, those watchwords have been repeated again and again. At the same time, open considerations of power — of what is involved in the actual prediction or the actual control of people — have been sparse in the social science literature. This is especially true of the literature that is closely associated with the academic establishment — the social science departments of the various universities, which rarely support either Freudians or Marxians.

The molding of the modern academic institution bears heavily on the question I am raising about the possibility of intervention by social science to ameliorate human problems. Following the Civil War, the United States experienced a great burst of urbanization and industrialization. Colleges and universities were needed, especially to promote science for both agriculture and manufacturing. The land grant colleges were established. The great industrial fortunes were used to establish new universities and to refurbish old ones. Many young Americans went to learn science in Europe, especially Germany, and came back to establish laboratories in the universities.

Psychology took the lead among the social sciences in attempting to model itself on the physical sciences. It thereby drew to itself a kind of administrative support that the classics and philosophy departments were not able to draw. John Watson had sounded the call. In the period from about just before World War I to World War II, psychology departments increasingly became behavioristic. Psychology radically separated itself from the humanities and aligned itself with the sciences. In due course it exorcised virtually all direct considerations of power from curricula and research. Perhaps the single dramatic exception to this trend were the studies by Kurt Lewin of the effects of democratic, autocratic and laissez-faire styles. But he restricted the studies to small groups, individual interactions, and laboratory-type situations, and did not consider the power structures of the larger society. Insofar as Lewin's studies reflected at all on the power structure of the larger society, they stood, at best, as parables. The concern with power remained the province of some of the literary Freudians and the Marxians, almost completely outside of the colleges and universities. Social psychology of the laboratory type, modeled after Lewin, could stand as no more than a token treatment by the psychologist of the topic of power in the society.

During World War II, it became evident that psychologists and other social scientists could somehow be extremely useful in connection with the increasingly complex sets of human factors with which the military were forced to deal. While the physical scientists were obviously very useful, having been closely associated with the atom bomb, radar, and the like, the social scientists also turned out to be eminently useful. The psychologists did remarkable things in connection with selection and training, the assessment of morale and opinion, analyses of such things as the interactions among members of bomber and others types of crews, design of man-operated equipment, techniques of interrogation, training of intelligence officers, and the like.

Following the war, there was a brief period of very high nervousness about the power held by the possessors of knowledge; there existed a great fear that their minds would be seduced or captured by potential enemies. McCarthy and the persecution of Oppenheimer exemplify the national nervousness of this time. Also around this time, the U.S. federal government became a major force in supporting and directing the civilian intellectual enterprises of colleges and especially universities. Programs supporting research were launched in virtually every imaginable factual area. These programs were very similar to other kinds of preparedness training. Thus, in order to maintain a pilot population, the government required pilots to fly a certain number of hours a month. Similarly, in order to maintain the science establishment, the government supported research of many kinds. But the supported projects were very tightly controlled to ensure satisfying what were considered to be the *scientific* criteria.

In the social sciences the federal government supported innumerable studies of co-occurrences, characteristically represented by tables and graphs showing the data from events in terms of two variables. Of course, there was great excitement associated with the introduction of analysis of variance, multiple correlations, and the like because of the promise of being able to deal with co-occurrence entailing more than two variables. At the same time, there was very little support given to research bearing directly on power. And certainly there was no support to society-oriented research informed in any way by Freudian or Marxian thought.

By the late 1950s and early 1960s the term "behavioral science" gained a certain amount of currency. Developments corresponding to the behavioristic movement in psychology were taking place in sociology, political science, economics, and even in law and psychiatry. Behavioralism, understood as the concentration of attention on overt human activity, restricted the major focus of researchers to the raw material of human behavior and to the identification of patterns of co-occurrence and became the major vocation of virtually all the academic social scientists. Behavioralism, as an ideology, aligned itself with those views calling themselves empirical and positivistic. The presumptive search for laws of human behavior came to be the search for patterns of co-occurrence among statistical measures that exceeded expectation based on normal variability, that is, so-called significant results. (For a collection of papers showing the numerous illogicalities associated with the application of the test of significance, see Morrison and Henkel, 1970.)

At the same time, an attitude of regarding phenomena as value free was required of investigators, young graduate students, and laboratory assistants. The intense separation of the pure from the applied was supported. The academic researcher was to devote himself to the pure. We can now understand *pure* as a euphemism for considerations that avoid the question of power. Pure research was supposed to concern itself with knowledge only and leave to others the questions of the power implicit in knowledge, as indicated in the Baconian maxim.

The main question that I am addressing, the question of the application of the social sciences to the solution of the larger social problems, is, in context of history, an impertinent question. And I would want to dwell on that word a bit. The word impertinent has two meanings. One denotes an unseemly intrusion, presumption, or insolence. My dictionary indicates that we understand the word as in the expression "an impertinent boy." It indicates that the word is synonymous with impudence, boldness, rudeness, and arrogance. The second meaning is not pertinent or not relevant. Concerning the relationship between the two meanings, the author of the dictionary entry says the following: "impertinent, from its primary meaning of not pertinent and hence inappropriate or out of place, has come to imply often an unseemly intrusion into what does not concern one, or a presumptuous rudeness toward one entitled to deference or respect: *an impertinent interruption, question, manner toward a teacher*" (*The American College Dictionary,* 1964, p. 607).

The history of the social sciences during the last hundred years, as I have outlined it, or the history of science going back at least to the granting of the charter to the Royal Society of London on condition of nonparticipation in political and religious affairs, is partly a history of how the raising of questions of application by scientists became an impertinence. That history entailed the formation of a complex of attitudes and beliefs into which scientists would be socialized as a condition for gaining the education, liberty, and resources needed for the pursuit of the scientific purpose. Scientists were given a specific place in the power structure. That place was combined with a particular conception of science; it would serve the double purpose of making it possible for scientists to make contributions to knowledge in a way that would be valuable to others, but not in a way that obviously bore on the critical power issues of the society.

A few words are in order about the very special and important case of the atom bomb. As is well known, early in World War II some physicists became aware that the making of an atom bomb was increasingly feasible. There was some slight evidence that suggested the Germans might already have seriously begun such an enterprise. Albert Einstein, whose public reputation was the highest among the group, was persuaded to send a letter to President Roosevelt, thus informing him. The assumption that a letter to Roosevelt from Einstein would at least be treated seriously and would be brought to the president's attention was confirmed. This resulted in the formation of the Manhattan Project, the eventual construction of atom bombs, and the bombings of Hiroshima and Nagasaki.

The Manhattan Project is an extremely important case in point of the issue I am discussing. It was conducted in profound secrecy. Although only a handful of the people knew the aim of the project, many scientists and technicians of various kinds worked on the project, solving difficult scientific and technical problems. The latter did not ask for, and were not told, reasons. They received the problems that were assigned to them and solved them.

The Manhattan Project demonstrated that the methods of division of labor could be applied to scientific and technical problems. But even more importantly, it clearly demonstrated that the radical separation of scientific research from its aims was not a handicap, and indeed provided the further advantage of security. The methods of division of labor and of the assembly line had certainly been successful in building cars and the like. But here it became evident that something like an assembly line approach could also be used for research and development. This discovery informed the subsequent programs of research supported by the government. With it came an even greater stress on the socialization of the scientific community.

### Revisiting David Hume and Joshua

Let us revisit David Hume and Joshua. Had a social scientist of a Humean persuasion been asked by Joshua to present him with a review of relevant literature, he might have been able, perhaps, to find a few studies that bore on it. Let us say the investigator reviewed forty critical battles in history and arranged the data in a chi-square table, a 2 × 3. Along the side, marking the rows, he wrote "victor" and "vanquished"; across the top, the three categories "advanced," "retreated," and "stood" — chi-square significant at, let us say, the 5 percent level, with the large cells being "victor-advanced" and "vanquished-retreated." A second investigation entailed showing persons from the city of Ai a set of pictures as in Murray's Thematic Apperception Test. These pictures represented a variety of battle situations, and the subject was asked to make up a story about them, to tell what happened prior to the event depicted in the picture, to tell what appears to be going on in the picture, and to indicate what will take place in the future. One of the pictures, the report indicates, shows a group of people running while another group of people are watching them run away. A very large proportion of the respondents, say 90 percent, interpret the runners as a vanquished army in retreat. Joshua and his lieutenants consider these reports. Someone proposes the strategy indicated in the Bible, and Joshua and the lieutenants discuss it. One suggests that, in view of the relatively large chi-square and the 5 percent p-value with that particular number of subjects in the study, they should aim for one of the low frequency cells—the "victor-retreated" cell—on the grounds that the king of Ai would not be likely to expect that. Another raises the question, what if the king of Ai is like one of the 10 percent of the respondents to the TAT-picture? Joshua says that with a 90 percent-10 percent split, and God's help, it is a risk they should take. The social scientist remains silent after having given his report, for otherwise he would be regarded by Joshua and the lieutenants as "impertinent." He is grateful that he is in on the council. And, if I may be permitted to be even more loose with history, he is grateful to the Humean indoctrination he received in graduate school, which brought him to such high places.

All of this is to ask whether the set of highly servile beliefs and attitudes that the community of scientists has adopted as presumptive aids in the pursuit of truth, and which have been transformed into canons of method, are not themselves disqualifying. For while change must necessarily confront power, there is implicit acceptance of the prevailing power arrangements built into that which is commonly taught and taken to be the scientific method. This is why I am pessimistic.

## The Future

At the outset of this presentation I indicated that I was both pessimistic and optimistic. Up till now I have generally indicated the grounds for my pessimism. I have outlined a condition in which the social scientist is essentially locked into a power system. The power system itself works to support the characteristic scientific ideology. That particular scientific ideology constitutes a design whereby the social scientist might be of service to power persons in the society, but essentially keeps him in a position of impotence. What then could constitute the grounds for any optimism? The grounds are essentially that the impotence of which I speak is hardly that firm, that the impotence yields in the face of light, and that the objective conditions are such that light has considerably greater advantages for all than the advantages that accrue to some from the darkness of others.

In the course of this discussion I have used a military example—Joshua and the Battle of Ai—to make some of my points. The choice of a military example to discuss power relations and intelligence is not fortuitous. I have chosen it, in part, in recognition of the fact that, at least historically, the ultimate theater in which power conflicts express themselves is warfare. But then, one might ask, why am I optimistic?

Perhaps it is only a shred of hope. I am prepared to see that the warfare context, which so conditions our lives, is also a source of hope. Let us allow that we Europeans—including most of the people in the Americas—are among the most warlike people in the history of the earth. The history of Western civilization is a history of virtually continuous warfare. It is a fact we regularly try to repress. Indeed, it can be argued that the very fact of repression is a critical part of the dynamic that makes us break out in warfare with almost predictable rhythms.

We have reached the point where the dangers of war are so great that they far outweigh any imaginable political, social, or economic advantages that might be reached by warfare. The steady improvement in the ability to hurl increasingly destructive things at each other with greater ranges and with greater accuracy than ever before makes it increasingly imprudent to try to solve the world's problems by such hurlings. If warfare were ever a prudent solution to a problem, a material or an existential problem, it no longer is. It might well be objected that my optimism is groundless, since it seems to be based on the assumption that people act prudently, not a very sound assumption.

But yet one other lesson learned from contemplating warfare may constitute a better ground for hope. That lesson is about the relationship between warfare and democracy. Why did democracy ever get started in the first place? Or, why did anyone who held power ever give it up to large groups of people who did not have it? Was the growth of democracy, wherever it took place, something that resulted just from the benevolence of the persons in power? Or did it derive from some kind of necessity? I suggest, at least if we might make any inferences at all from our observations concerning the nature of power, that few people who had power ever gave it up simply out of benign motives.

The theory has been advanced that democracy arose out of necessity, and in connection with warfare. According to this view—advanced by Max Weber (1958), among others—democracy was born in ancient Greece in connection with a change in the style of warfare. Prior to about 700 B.C., warfare was essentially a kind of knightly conflict between heroic warriors. Militarily capable men could claim the support and subordination of people by offering them protection. And when conflicts broke out, the conflicts were essentially of one such man of valor against another. These military men came to constitute an aristocracy and became the lords of their people.

But somewhere around 700 B.C. the style of warfare changed from individual combat to group battles. It was found that even a loosely coordinated large group of men could be militarily superior to the single hero, no matter how capable or how well equipped with weapons and horse. The phalanx, a group of men standing shoulder to shoulder and row behind row, could be superior to both the mounted warrior or the chariot. Because the safety of a community came to depend on a large number of people, the power in the community came to be more widely distributed. Indeed, it is this historical condition which informed the second amendment to the United States Constitution, which provides for the right to keep and bear arms.

80

In this example, there is a lesson that goes beyond the concrete historical circumstance having to do with physical protection and arms. The more
general form of the lesson, and the form in which it is applicable to the contemporary world situation, is in terms of good will and good judgment. Democracy depends on the good will and the good judgment of the citizenry at
large. Insofar as the society at large depends on the good will and the good
judgment of the individual, each individual in the society must have his or her
rights respected.

No amount of policing can adequately control a modern urban industrial society. The polity, the economy, and the society as a whole cannot function without the eminent good will and the good judgment of virtually every-
body in the society. I believe that the totalitarian governments of recent history—from Frederick the Great's Prussia to Napoleon's Empire, to those of the
twentieth century—have simply become anachronistic. Not even the armed
forces can function on the basis of obedience and centralized command any-
more. The nature of modern warfare has become such that every soldier has to
be capable of thinking like a commander and be willing to do so. The fact is
that democracy has become an increasingly necessary condition for the society
to function. Democracy is not, as we have sometimes thought about it, a lux-
ury, or a reward, or that which one wins from war. Democracy is a major condition for survival and more an instrument of protection than something that
requires protection.

What then is the role of the social scientist? In such a context man's
understanding of himself becomes increasingly important. The work of the
social scientist is to contribute to the growth of that understanding.

## References

Arendt, H. *The Human Condition.* Chicago: University of Chicago Press, 1958.
Morrison, D. E., and Henkel, R. E. (Eds.). *The Significance Test Controversy.* Chicago:
    Aldine, 1970.
Weber, M. *The Protestant Ethic and the Spirit of Capitalism.* (T. Parsons, Trans.) New York:
    Scribners, 1958.

*David Bakan is professor of psychology at
York University, Ontario.*

*Psychology's lack of acceptance in the public domain underlies its widespread, current politicization.*

# Psychology: The Unwanted Science

## Irwin Silverman

To avoid conversations in which I am likely to be drawn to a defense of my profession, I sometimes tell outright lies to seatmates in airplanes and others who ask me what I do for a living. On one occasion, when I did not, I had the following exchange with an otherwise pleasant lady, on the topic of the frustration-aggression relationship in child development.

"Well," she said, "in response to the data, I have a son who always had whatever he wanted and he is as nasty to me as he can be."

I replied in my best introductory psychology pedagogy. "He may have experienced frustration in ways that you didn't recognize, or something else might be the cause. Frustration isn't the only thing that causes aggression, but it is one."

She digested this for a few seconds, then shook her head. "Spare the rod and spoil the child. You may be a doctor and all that, but I've raised three children, and that much I know for sure."

Of course, if I was a biologist or physicist, I could have told her that blueberries cause blindness, or that the earth is really much flatter than we thought, and received a respectful nod. About our bodies and physical environments, we readily yield to scientific experts, but behavior is another matter.

Our awareness of these attitudes is reflected in our introductory texts, which traditionally open with lengthy, self-conscious passages on the right of psychology to call itself a science; poke fun at the foibles of conventional wisdom; or describe how behavioral scientists think and act in the same ways as other scientists. In contrast, I have never found a textbook in the natural sciences that carries a line defending the credentials of the field.

The faith of the populace was not a birthright of the natural sciences. Every discipline shouldered its way past popular skepticism; not, however, by rhetoric, but by generating visible, substantial, enduring products. Psychology has provided virtually nothing in this regard. Probably the closest to one, in the public eye, is the clinical enterprise; but this is generally viewed as a technical arm of psychiatry, and psychiatry is suffering its own well-deserved identity crisis.

Psychology's lack of product is often ascribed to its status as an "infant science," an argument that remains somewhat credible, but paled considerably as we passed our centennial in 1979. More substantive analyses have tended to fault the pseudo-knowledge proliferated by misguided attempts to fit our concepts and methods precisely within the laboratory models of extant experimental disciplines. Cited, in particular, are the shortsighted assumptions that the responses of human subjects in the brief, mysterious, intimidating events termed psychological experiments had very much to do with the rest of their lives, and that the effects of their extraneous motives and intentions could be curtailed as simply as a biologist may curtail the effects of extraneous bacteria in his test tube. I was such a critic, and one of those who sounded the call for unobtrusive methods—experiments in the field and the like—which would move us toward data that were naturalistic, generalizable, and free from the illusion of precise manipulation, measurement, and control inherent in the standard psychological laboratory. As I approached the conclusion of my major effort on this topic (Silverman, 1977a), I proceeded to try to practice what I had preached.

I had a theory that pertained to a then lively question within social psychology: Why do bystanders to dangerous emergencies frequently not provide indirect aid (for example, phoning police, even anonymously, to report a mugging)? I believed my theory and, more to the point, I felt that it led gracefully to a series of trenchant hypotheses, amenable to tightly controlled, unobtrusive experiments. These required that I provoke fairly intense conflicts in subjects, who were not aware they were part of an experiment, between their desires to directly aid an acutely suffering victim and their anxieties about dangerous consequences to themselves. Interestingly, I had only minor problems with ethics committees, but once pilot studies were in progress, and effective manipulations were found, I faced major problems with the consciences (or whatever) of my graduate student collaborators and myself. I presented the theory here and there (Silverman, 1974, 1975) with references to my dilemma about putting it to proper test. Some others, who were writing on the same question that spawned the theory, seemed to like it very much, but none accepted my open invitation to do the experiments. It would have been, I feel, my most cogent research endeavor, both from conceptual and utilitarian standpoints. I never did have ethical problems with my less cogent endeavors.

Eventually, I came to the conclusion that my dilemma was a reflection of a pressing, general problem for psychological experimentation, at least in those areas that trade in molar social, developmental, and personality variables (Silverman, 1977b). We need to be unobtrusive. At the same time, we often need experimental manipulanda with meaningful impact on subjects if their responses are to lead to meaningful conclusions about meaningful events. It is a constraining combination. Some of our number, such as Milgram (1963) and Zimbardo and his colleagues (1973) have pushed past the constraints with compelling yields. (Although Zimbardo's study was not unobtrusive in the sense that subjects were aware they were subjects, the manipulanda were of sufficient impact and duration to compensate.) Their films are probably the most frequently presented in introductory courses; their articles, the most frequently reprinted in undergraduate readers. It is significant, however, that in both cases the reactions within the field dealt at least as much with the ethics of the research as with the importance of the findings; and both investigators stated that they, themselves, did not expect their subjects to respond as intensely as they did. It is an open question whether they would have proceeded had they anticipated this intense response, although the latter study was prematurely concluded for this reason.

The great majority of us tend to limit ourselves to deliberately innocuous analogues of the processes we aspire to generalize. Perhaps my airplane seatmate expressed a valid intuition. Did we ever believe that the minor frustrations induced in laboratory and field experiments produced more than minor, momentary dispositions to aggression? If we did, we probably would not have condoned the research. How confident can we be, then, in our generalizations about child-rearing practices, economic cycles, minority-group prejudice, and the like.

Nevertheless, I do not believe that either methodological or ethical considerations are the primary reasons for our lack of product. Natural scientists face problems of the same general order, and psychologists are not inferior in the ingenuity required to surmount these problems. A more salient factor is that there is virtually no public market for psychology's products. Whenever we have extended them, they have been rejected or ignored. Consider some examples through the decades.

One can scarcely find a reference to subliminal stimulation in contemporary texts, but it was a popular item in the 1950s, with dramatic implications for covert, mass influence. Despite subsequent demurrers that it probably does not work anyway (Bugelski, 1973), there was compelling evidence in its favor (Cooper, 1979; Dixon, 1971); so compelling, in fact, that the Federal Communications Commission of the United States was moved to ban its use in the public media (Cooper, 1979).

The 1960s was the era of cognitive dissonance theory. At the height of interest, no less a news source than the *New York Times Magazine* carried an article (Aronson, 1966) that persuasively described subtle, counterintuitional proscriptions for controlling the attitudinal development of the very young, based on sound, replicated, long-term research. The article provoked a passionate reply from a reader, published several weeks later, decrying the Orwellian implications of the possible discovery of scientific means for molding the value systems of subsequent generations. I assume that most of the millions of readers who followed the exchange shared my own sympathies with that letter, for I have observed no dissonance-oriented trends in parenting since 1966, and I cannot even find a reference to it in Spock.

The 1970s witnessed the full wrath of the world's foremost consumer advocate, Ralph Nader, upon the educational testing movement, the one area in which psychologists have provided anything approximating a public product (*APA Monitor,* November 1976). The full consequences of Nader's attack remain to be seen, but the state of California, generally a pioneer of social trends, has already outlawed the use of IQ scores to classify school children.

The reasons for public disavowal of behavioral science products are probably evident from the illustrations. The application of scientific data inexorably implies control of natural processes. For psychology, these processes can be described as thought, feeling, and behavior; often, the mechanisms of control are necessarily covert, as in subliminal stimulation and the manipulation of cognitive dissonance. Psychology's products will frequently, then, represent blatant violations of the most revered concept of free will. Even when control is overt (for example, classification by IQ tests), psychologists confront an obstacle peculiar to the discipline. The public-at-large will accept the imposition òf science when there are commonly held goals to be served. These are abundant in the natural sciences; health, longevity, communication, and transportation are instances. There are virtually none where psychological processes are concerned. There are only divergent, vested interests.

There are concepts that appear to reflect universal, behavioral goals, but, on closer examination, these generally prove to be merely apparent. Mental health is a case in point. Applications of the term invariably reflect personal or social ideologies, and so-called universal definitions are sufficiently encompassing to incorporate any of these. In perhaps the most widely used abnormal psychology text throughout its five editions, Coleman (1976) defines mental health, quite typically, in terms of behavior that "fosters the well-being of the individual and ultimately the group" (p. 15). Western clinicians seemed surprised and offended in the mid-1970s to learn that, within these strictures, their counterparts in the Soviet Union had quite different criteria for mental health or the lack of it. A good education may be another: however, what you mean by this will be very different, depending on whether you endorse the goals of B. F. Skinner or Erik Erikson. The objections of Nader's group and the state of California to classification by IQ tests were also a reflection of conflicting social values: the question is whether the rights of the individual take precedence over potential benefits to the majority.

The lack of an applied role in the public domain deprives psychology of the sweeping benefits that obtain with popular demand for scientific products. Biology might still be a tentative endeavor, were it not for the informational needs and applications of the health-related professions. The splitting of the atom was accomplished within the province of basic research, but it remained a laboratory oddity for nearly ten years, and emerged to herald the era of nuclear physics with the race for a super weapon during World War II. By the same token, the findings of Milgram and Zimbardo and his colleagues remain laboratory oddities, despite their profound implications about the socialization experiences that permit the ascendance of malevolent authority. Milgram's notions about the deterrent effects of selective disobedience training will never find a natural laboratory for their development, probably because we could not obtain a consensual definition of malevolent authority except within the confines of an experiment, nor could we arrive at a ratio to describe the optimal, tolerable degree of general anarchy that may be a byproduct of disobedience training.

It follows, naturally, that psychology's principal applications are by vested interests and without publicity. Evidence by a Canadian source (Key, 1972) suggests that visual subliminal stimulation is apparently successfully used in the public media by advertisers outside of the reach of United States law, and several investigative newspaper reports (Egelhof, 1978; Peterson, 1977; Ward, 1980) have revealed that an auditory device has found wide usage in retail stores, factories, and real estate offices throughout the world. Although the tenets of dissonance theory did not become part of parenting lore, they were rapidly incorporated into the jargon of the marketing and public relations worlds. Industrial psychologists enjoy a burgeoning demand for their skills, although I am certain that industrial workers would not appreciate techniques based on the Hawthorne effect or on other discoveries about how to increase productivity by covert methods. Even if Ralph Nader accomplishes his mission to remove psychological testing from the public educational system, it will continue to occupy a prominent place in the private sector, where users are less constrained by issues of individual rights and more tolerant of Type II errors.

Paradoxically, the diffidence of the populace toward psychological products is matched by the eagerness of psychologists to gain entry into the public arena. One result of this eagerness to be useful is that we have occasionally been drawn into a sociopolitical role, at some compromise to our scientific role. More often than not, the causes we served were commensurate with our generally liberal, humanitarian leanings, and it is difficult to quarrel with the social benefits of the results. Certainly, no right-thinking person will fail to recognize the odiousness of minority group segregation, nor fail to realize, intuitively, that such discrimination is bound to produce deleterious effects on the victims. Thus the obvious pride of social psychologists in their role in the United States Supreme Court decision on desegregation in 1954 can be readily appreciated. If we view psychology's role in terms of pure academic considerations, however, we might be forced to admit that the conclusions we presented about the effects of school segregation on motivation and learning ability, based on descriptive data, interviews and projective tests (Clark, 1953), represented much more of an interpretive leap than our stringent rules of evidence customarily permit. Similarly, in 1975 a veritable horde of psychologists accepted invitations to testify before a commission of the Canadian government on the "cause-effect relationship" between violence in the communications media, "and the incidence of violent crime in society" (Report of the Ontario Royal Commission on Violence, p. 50). From the unequivocal conclusion of the commission, it is apparent that few, if any, of our number took the position that the available, ambiguous results of experiments that were microcosmic analogues of the question were unsuited to such a generalization. I suspect that most would have been far more critical had the interpretation been voiced in a journal article they were reviewing or an oral dissertation they were attending. Nevertheless, if this exercise leads to a diminution of television violence, probably most of us, as concerned members of society, will feel gratified and proud of our contribution. Our self-concepts as members of the scientific community, however, may take a different turn.

Psychology has become increasingly politicized, to the point where it seems to be all-encompassing. Trends in areas of public concern, such as the environment and women's rights, are now followed almost instantaneously by the creation of new subfields within the discipline, complete with journals and American Psychological Association divisions. Committees of the association are forming for the expressed purpose of establishing inroads into public policy. The *APA Monitor* reads more like the newsletter of a Congressional lobby than a scientific organization. In our universities, basic research courses and programs remain stagnant at best while those of an applied nature seem to grow progressively, despite the absence of any breakthroughs to justify the transition. And finally, in disregard for the total lack of homogeneity of underlying theories and practices in the products we do offer, particularly in the area of clinical psychology, we devote massive efforts and funds to protect and extend our legal claims to exclusivity as licensed behavior experts. The fact that two state governments have recently refused to renew their licensing laws for this reason (and that others are taking the matter under review) suggests that our public relations have begun to surpass our credibility.

In its perennial search for identity and respectability, psychology appears to be abandoning the model of the physical sciences. Certainly biologists and physicists comport themselves with proper scientific conservatism and taciturnity when meeting informational demands of the public. Their tendency is to avoid unwarranted generalizations in applying research findings, even at the sacrifice of some that may, in fact, be valid. Psychology is taking the opposite tack, seemingly to the point of proselytizing. Our new role model seems to be the political pressure group.

Psychology's new political face may increase our visibility by making us more readily available for the propaganda purposes of various interest groups, virtuous or otherwise, but it can only detract from the quality of the science and perhaps eventually erode whatever popular credibility we may have. Further, the movement toward social relevance appears to have eclipsed and confounded the efforts toward conceptual relevance that had gained a solid footing with the revelations about the social psychology of the psychological experiment of the mid-1960s to 1970s. Within the latter movement, the purpose of research in life settings was to enhance the relevance of psychological data to the constructs to which they were intended to pertain. This is quite a separate issue from the relevance of data to social problems (Silverman, 1971), though the two concerns are often regarded as synonymous by both advocates and critics of the politicizing of psychology.

By the nature of its subject matter, psychology has always been vulnerable to becoming political, but the upsurge of the 1970s seems largely based on pragmatic considerations — the attrition of job opportunities and funding at all levels for basic research in the social sciences that inevitably accompanies economic recession. Thus, it is naive to expect that the tide will be turned by polemics. It is heartening, however, to believe that the trend represents part of a cycle, and eventually we will resume, en masse, our appropriate mission: the untrammeled and uncompromising search for laws of behavior.

This return will probably require that we lose much of our self-consciousness about who wants us and who does not. A science can survive and even flourish without mass acclaim for products. Astronomy is a case in point. Ethology is another. True, these are not deprived of a natural laboratory, as are many areas of psychology, but it is adaptive for us to recognize our constraints and find the means to work and progress within them, rather than to court public acceptance at whatever cost to scientific goals and integrity.

## References

Aronson, E. "Try a Little Dissonance." *New York Times Magazine,* September 11, 1966.

Bugelski, R. B. *An Introduction to the Principles of Psychology.* (2nd ed.) Indianapolis, Ind.: Bobbs-Merrill, 1973.

Clark, K. B. "The Social Scientist as an Expert Witness in Civil Rights Litigation." *Social Problems,* 1953, *1,* 5–10.

Coleman, J. C. *Abnormal Psychology and Modern Life.* (5th ed.) Glenview, Ill.: Scott, Foresman, 1976.

Cooper, E. F. "Subliminal Perception and Advertising: Background Information and Bibliography." *Library of Congress: Congressional Research Service Report,* No. 79–577, April 9, 1979.

Dixon, N. F. *Subliminal Perception: The Nature of a Controversy.* New York: McGraw-Hill, 1971.

Egelhof, J. "Furor Rises over Possibility of Sneaking Ads into Mind." *Chicago Tribune,* August 18, 1978, p. 4.

Key, W. B. *Subliminal Seduction.* Englewood Cliffs, N.J.: Prentice-Hall, 1972.

Milgram, S. "Behavioral Study of Obedience." *Journal of Abnormal and Social Psychology,* 1963, *67,* 371–378.

Peterson, J. "Ads That Try to Get Inside Your Head." *National Observer,* February 26, 1977, pp. 1, 15.

*Report of the Ontario Royal Commission on Violence in the Communications Industry.* Vol. 1. Toronto: Ministry of Government Services, 1976.

Silverman, I. "Crisis in Social Psychology: The Relevance of Relevance." *American Psychologist,* 1971, *26,* 583–584.

Silverman, I. "Some Hedonistic Considerations Regarding Altruistic Behavior." Paper presented to the Southeastern Psychological Association, Miami, 1974.

Silverman, I. "The Bystander Effect: Some Alternative Interpretations." Paper presented to the Eastern Psychological Association, New York, 1975.

Silverman, I. *The Human Subject in the Psychological Laboratory.* Elmsford, N.Y.: Pergamon Press, 1977a.

Silverman, I. "Why Social Psychology Fails." *Canadian Psychological Review,* 1977b, *18,* 353–358.

Ward, O. "The Message that Mellows Your Mind." *Toronto Star,* October 26, 1980.

Zimbardo, P., and others. "A Pirandellian Prison." *New York Times Magazine,* April 8, 1975.

*Irwin Silverman is professor of psychology,*
*York University, Ontario.*

# Index

# New Directions Quarterly Sourcebooks

*New Directions for Methodology of Social and Behavioral Science* is one of several distinct series of quarterly sourcebooks published by Jossey-Bass. The sourcebooks in each series are designed to serve both as *convenient compendiums* of the latest knowledge and practical experience on their topics and as *long-life reference tools*.

One-year, four-sourcebook subscriptions for each series cost $18 for individuals (when paid by personal check) and $30 for institutions, libraries, and agencies. Single copies of earlier sourcebooks are available at $6.95 each *prepaid* (or $7.95 each when *billed*).

A complete listing is given below of current and past sourcebooks in the *New Directions for Methodology of Social and Behavioral Science* series. The titles and editors-in-chief of the other series are also listed. To subscribe, or to receive further information, write: New Directions Subscriptions, Jossey-Bass Inc., Publishers, 433 California Street, San Francisco, California 94104.

*New Directions for Methodology of Social and Behavioral Science*
Donald W. Fiske, Editor-in-Chief

1979–1980:　1. *Unobtrusive Measurement Today,* Lee Sechrest
　　　　　　2. *Methods for Studying Person-Situation Interactions,*
　　　　　　　Lynn R. Kahle
　　　　　　3. *Realizations of Brunswik's Representative Design,*
　　　　　　　Kenneth R. Hammond, Nancy E. Wascoe
　　　　　　4. *Fallible Judgment in Behavioral Research,*
　　　　　　　Richard A. Shweder
1980–1981:　5. *Quantitative Assessment of Research Domains,*
　　　　　　　Robert Rosenthal
　　　　　　6. *Issues in Aggregation,* Karlene H. Roberts,
　　　　　　　Leigh Burstein
　　　　　　7. *Biopolitics: Ethological and Physiological Approaches,*
　　　　　　　Meredith W. Watts

*New Directions for Child Development*
William Damon, Editor-in-Chief

*New Directions for College Learning Assistance*
Kurt V. Lauridsen, Editor-in-Chief

*New Directions for Community Colleges*
Arthur M. Cohen, Editor-in-Chief
Florence B. Brawer, Associate Editor